Margar
from Betty Hambly
(née Cadbury)
1996

C000097734

To Lucy Bellows
our Mother
and her descendants

COVER DESIGN – *John Bellows looking at The Birdlip Mirror, which is of bronze, incised and enamalled: Iron Age circa 25 AD. It was found in a grave near Birdlip, Gloucestershire, in 1879, bought by John Bellows and presented to Gloucester City Museum, its present location.*

John Bellows in Quaker dress in 1891

A Many-Sided Man

JOHN BELLOWS

of Gloucester

1831 to 1902

Quaker Printer, Lexicographer and Archaeologist

– His Life and Letters –

by

Kate Charity

With an additional chapter by
Malcolm J. Watkins, Archaeology Director,
City of Gloucester Museum

William Sessions Limited
York, England

ISBN 1 85072 132 7

1993 © Dr Katharine M. Charity

Printed in 11 on 12 point Plantin Typeface from Author's disk
by William Sessions Limited
The Ebor Press, York, England

Contents

Chapter   *Page*

    Genealogy viii

    Preface ix

  I Forbears and Early Life 1

  II Gloucester 7

  III A Winter Journey and The Dictionary 10

  IV Marriage and *The Track of the War around Metz* ... 20

  V Peace, Printing and Pamphlets 30

  VI Quakers, Ireland and Family Life 39

  VII Russia, The Caucasian Exiles 53

  VIII Tolstoy and the Doukhabors 71

  IX Letters, Bulgaria, Peace Conference 84

  X The Boer War 93

  XI The Last Journey, the USA, Harvard, Illness and Death 97

    Epilogue 109

    Appendix I: Archaeology by Malcolm J. Watkins ... 113

    Appendix II: A list of John Bellows's Writings ... 119

    Bibliography 122

    Index 124

Illustrations

Page

John Bellows in Quaker Dress in 1891 ... ... *frontispiece*

From a contemporary cartoon vii

Birthplace at Liskeard, Cornwall 1

Lisburn School – about 1850 3

Map showing Winter journey to Norway and back 13

French Dictionary manuscript with corrections ... 18 and 19

Elizabeth Earnshaw, 1862 20

Handlow House, Churcham, near Gloucester 21

John Bellows in the late 1860's 22

Map of Metz 24

A war-ruined house 26

Gloucester Printing Works, 1882 32

Gloucester Printing Works c.1920s/1930s 32

Bellows' Rapid Wages Cylinder ... ... 34 and 35

John Bellows' drawing of Montpesat 38

Upton Knoll House – sketch by George Charity 40

Severn Railway Bridge 40

Family picnic – late 1880s 44

Oliver Wendell Holmes 51

Map of Caucasus 52

Caucasus Travelling Trio 55

Mount Kasbek... 62

Dangerous mountain path 62

Hotel d'Angleterre, St Petersburg – John Burrows 72

The Tolstoy family 73

Hannah Bellows in Manitoba, Canada 83

The Bellows family, 1890's 85

Frederick Sessions 96

John and Elizabeth on board ship 98

Elizabeth Bellows, 1893 105

John, Elizabeth and Lucy Bellows 108

The Birdlip Grave Group ... ... 116 and 117

"RESOLVED THAT IN FUTURE DEATH ALONE SHOULD
PART US FROM BELLOWS' DICTIONARY."

From a contemporary cartoon

The Bellows Genealogy – 19th & 20th Centuries

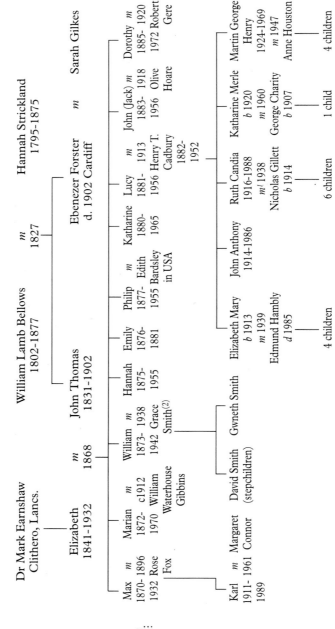

Preface

THIS ACCOUNT OF THE LIFE of my grandfather, John Bellows, is based largely on the Memoir and Letters compiled by Elizabeth, his wife, shortly after his death. Their children, especially their youngest son, Jack, also kept many letters, newspaper cuttings, etc., and from these sources I have tried to suggest both the flavour of John's personality and the broad pattern of his life, using his own writing wherever possible.

He died some 18 years before I was born so, of course, I never met him; but I do remember my grandmother and her home, Tuffley Lawn, where she lived with three of her children. She must have been nearly 90, and I have a clear recollection of a frail, gentle old lady, sitting up in bed in a quiet darkened room.

★   ★   ★

I would like to thank all those who have encouraged me to write the book, especially my husband, George, who has patiently supported me in every way, not only by typing the original manuscript on his ancient Olympia machine, but also by following the book's progress. We have both found that getting to know John has been a revealing and rewarding exercise. I am grateful for the keen and committed interest of my sister Betty Hambly: for the attic archives of my cousin, Margaret Bellows, and to both for their invaluable family recollections.

I am most grateful, too, to those who have spurred me on from the start, particularly Althea Boyack and Margaret Maxwell who read the script with a critical eye: to Millicent Stead and Delia Huddy who have kindly given me their professional advice: to Judith Batchelor for indexing: to Brian Boothby who took such care to reproduce photographs, and to those who have given permission to use them.

I am also indebted to Malcolm Watkins, the Gloucester Museum's Archaeological Curator, who has always shown interest in John Bellows and has willingly assessed John's archaeological finds in the context of present-day knowledge: to Arthur Chapman and the Governors of the Friends School, Lisburn for permission to quote from 'The History of the School': to the Librarians of the Friends House Library and the Gloucester Reference Library for their assistance; to Janet MacPhail for her patience and skill in word-processing the book: to my daughter, Ruth, for her constructive suggestions and, of course, to William and Margaret Sessions for their constant reassuring guidance and to both them and their staff for their professional skills.

To John Bellows
'The Modern Caxton'

I'm pleased to hear you've ta'en a
        comely wife,
Like other prudent, honest fellows,
And may you be, through all a lengthened
        life,
A loving, happy pair of Bellows.

While others, at this joyous nuptial
        time,
May send you gold or silver dishes,
I've naught to give beside the simple
        rhyme,
And very best of human wishes.

        H.Y.J.T.

Gloucester Journal, February 6th, 1869

CHAPTER I

Forbears and Early Life

WHEN JOHN BELLOWS WAS CYCLING through Cornwall with his two eldest sons, he described his place of birth in a letter to his wife,

"As we went up to our rooms, both of which faced into the little narrow Church Street, it seemed as though a tall man might have leaned out of the window and touched the panes of glass of the grocer's shop opposite (kept by Mr. Bevan). With a stick I certainly could have done so. I did not know till this morning when Mary Elliott most kindly walked down the street with me after Meeting to show me the spot, that my room was next door to the house in which I was born, and the street I was so amused with as a sort of doll's roadway was the very one upon which my baby wonderment had first looked down long years ago."

Birthplace at Liskeard, Cornwall

John Thomas Bellows was born at Carthew House, Church Street, Liskeard, Cornwall, on January 18th, 1831. His parents, William and Hannah Bellows, had moved there in 1829, two years after their marriage in Dorset in 1827. William, a native of Bere Regis, between Dorchester and Poole, was descended from Nonconformist stock on both sides of his family. (His

1

maternal ancestor, Philip Lamb, was deprived of his living as a Vicar of Bere Regis, after the Act of Uniformity was passed in 1662.) William was a well-educated man, a Hebrew scholar sufficiently proficient to teach that language, and, as is noted on John's birth certificate, earned his living as a schoolmaster. William was, clearly, a man of serious cast of mind, given to writing religious tracts, and a respected lay preacher of the Wesleyan connection.

Hannah was eight years his senior. Her father, John Strickland, had worked as Bailiff and Steward for the Bond family at Earthorne, near Wareham, where Hannah grew up. She was, evidently, an independently-minded girl for she had been "tempted to atheism" in her youth but, later, was attracted by the "plain speech and dress" of the Quaker, Stephen Grellett*.

It was probably through Hannah's Quaker interest that she and William became known to the Forster family of Bradpole, near Bridport in Dorset, with whom they formed a lasting friendship; and, when their second son was born, they named him "Ebenezer Forster" as a token of their affection. As a boy John had vivid memories of visits to the Forster's home and of playing with the well-kept toys of their only son who, by now, had grown up and left home. This son, William Edward Forster, later married the daughter of Dr. Thomas Arnold and, on "marrying out", left the Society of Friends. William became Liberal M.P. for Bradford, and was best known as the statesman who steered through Parliament the Elementary Education Bill in 1870 which brought about universal State education.

It was, undoubtedly, partly due to the influence of the Forster family that William and Hannah Bellows joined the Society of Friends in 1838. In the following year William applied for a post at the Friends School Lisburn, in Northern Ireland, whence the family moved after his successful application. At the time of William's appointment, the school was going through an unstable period, with staff problems. A record of the state of affairs in 1840 noted "serious

---

* Stephen Grellett de Mabilion: French aristocrat and Roman Catholic, turned Quaker. A powerful speaker, - known to have ministered to Cornish miners and elsewhere in Britain, as well as Europe and Russia.

difficulties have arisen from a spirit of insubordination and disobedience having shown itself ...... harmony can be restored only by administering discipline with a strict and temperate hand".

Alas, this was not William's forte: he was temperate, and his gentle, scholarly nature was not adapted to coping with rumbustious and undisciplined children, who were, clearly, out of hand. Unfortunately, by June 1841 the boys were so wild that it was thought best "to return them home both on account of repairs and of William and Hannah Bellows making request to be released as they had prospect of another situation". Later the school gradually returned to its original good standing.

At the school's centenary, John Bellows wrote,

".... of course my recollections of Prospect Hill are those of a child, for I was but seven or eight years old, which means that I remember things of small importance, and forget those of real weight. When I first knew the school, the boys wore no caps at play, but were like the London bluecoat scholars, bare-headed.

Lisburn School – about 1850

3

When a long country walk filled up a half-holiday, all the boys were marched through the housekeeper's room to be fitted with hats, or, to speak more accurately, to receive hats that did not fit. These were kept in two enormous baskets, and included patterns certainly dating from the last century. As we made a few changes, boy-like, after emerging into the yard below, for the sheer purpose of getting the very largest hats on the heads of the very smallest boys, and vice-versa, the effect was disreputable ...... In the playground we were not allowed to go out of bounds or to climb trees, and some of the minor exercises of discipline were for breaches of these rules. I remember my father one day finding a boy climbing a tree near the house, and the latter urged as a plea for the act, that he might grow up "a good Friend" and have a concern to travel in America as a minister, and that in such case his very life might depend on his being able to climb trees when chased by bears or other wild animals. I do not recollect how far this view availed with the master, but the boy knew his weak side, for he certainly wished the boys to grow up "good Friends".

It would have disheartened him, with this in mind, had he been aware that the boys of Prospect Hill, after several skirmishes with the town boys of Lisburn, accepted a challenge from the latter to fight out the cause of their quarrel in a pitched battle, and that they fixed the next Monthly Meeting day for the contest, because the master would be at Belfast attending it, and therefore out of the way. I was too small a boy to take part in the struggle, which I watched from behind a tree......

The most pleasant times of all to look back upon were, I think, the occasional holiday walks in the country. Moorland and mountain scenes again come to mind as I recall some of these ...."

The Bellows family must have been relieved to return to Cornwall, where William started a small school in Camborne for the children of the many Friends who lived there. His own boys were among the pupils, and William was much more successful this time in controlling and teaching his classes. One pupil, still living in 1904, spoke of him with much tenderness and even veneration.

John later recalled his life at home in Camborne through memories of the family cats.

4

"I have always been fond of them from a boy, when we had several generations of white Angoras. They were wonderfully affectionate creatures. One of them always climbed on to my mother's shoulder every morning as she came down to breakfast, and greeted her with a long side-rub against her right cheek, and then one on her left, after which she descended to the usual quadrupedal level. I came down one morning to find one of these lovely white cats on the table with her head in the cream jug. On hearing my approach I suppose she pricked up her ears, with the result that she could not withdraw herself from the jug. So she backed to the edge of the table and dropped, jug and all, to the floor. Here, lifting her head despairingly in the air, a stream of cream ran down her chest, and then, wildly bumping the encumbrance on the carpet, the china broke, but so as to leave the rim and handle as a collar round her neck as she fled from the room in shame .....

..... The daughter or granddaughter of our first white cat used to follow my father and mother for a mile along the road when they were walking from East Pool (Cornwall) to Redruth. This dear pussy met with a hard fate. Our house was near East Pool Mine, and the white cat was seen by the miners killing rats there. They are a superstitious set of men and believed that the killing of rats was the way to drive 'luck' from a mine. And so they killed our cat.

We children brought home her dead body, and gave it as impressive a funeral as we knew how. The nearest thing to Westminster Abbey that we had was a trellised summer-house in a corner of the garden, paved with white pebbles. The paving was taken up, and a grave dug in the centre, and then amid many tears her mortal remains were laid to rest."

When John was 14 he was apprenticed to Llewellyn Newton, a Camborne printer, who also kept a lending library. His indentures show that he was paid 2/- per week in his first year, thereafter rising by 1/- per week each year. There was a proviso, no doubt inserted by his father, that he would attend Quaker Meeting every Sunday. His boss was a considerate man, a leading Methodist in the town, who encouraged him to use the library as much as he liked. John's opportunities for reading were few, so he trained himself to read rapidly as he walked long distances on errands for his employer.

Among his "travelling companions" were Scott's novels and poetry, but, gradually, he developed a conscientious objection to works of fiction and stopped reading this kind of writing entirely. He joined the Camborne Mechanic's Institute and made use of its library and lectures. He gained some notoriety by writing a poem satirising a Roman Catholic movement that was attracting some attention; as a result of this satire, a Catholic lady invited him to dinner and, since he was curious, he overcame his mother's misgivings and accepted the invitation. Several other people were there, including a foreign priest, and John was flattered and was offered the chance of further education by the Catholics. This he rejected, probably because acceptance might have implied he was prepared to consider conversion.

In 1851 he moved to London, where he first found employment with Barrett & Sons, of Mark Lane, but his indentures were one year short of the requisite seven. It was a custom in Cornwall - and perhaps elsewhere - to back-date indentures by a year, but John's father refused to be a party to this shady practice: hence the difficulties that arose. A 'chapel' was convened and John was required to serve the extra year. This he firmly refused to do: instead, he found employment for six months with Harrisons, the Queen's printers. After which, finding London life little to his taste, he returned to Cornwall; but not for long. He soon accepted the offer of work as a foreman in a small business in Gloucester.

CHAPTER II

Gloucester

ON ARRIVING IN GLOUCESTER John found himself in a busy, prosperous and expanding city. The canal carrying river traffic between Sharpness and Gloucester had been completed, bringing timber and corn to the docks; flour mills and oil mills were built in the dock area, itself, and the Morelands Match factory was established in the Bristol Road. Furthermore, there was now a reasonable railway system linking Gloucester with other parts of the country. A population of 14,000 in 1841 increased to 40,000 in 1871. These factors, and many others, combined to make it an attractive place for an enterprising young printer.

For the first seven years John was employed by Mr. Wait, grocer's stationer; his work was to oversee the printing shop, which was staffed mainly by women. The firm was situated in Lower Westgate Street in a low-lying area known as The Island. In 1852 it was severely flooded and access was only possible by boat. During the emergency John, as foreman, had to remain on the premises. Although he thoroughly enjoyed the situation, his poor next-door neighbour was in great distress in her isolation, he was able, however, to help her by passing provisions, tied to a broomhandle, across to her window.

For two or three years he shared lodgings with his friend, Frederick Sessions, who, in an obituary appreciation, wrote, "We were the most intimate companions, sharing each others spiritual struggles, intellectual endeavours, social employments and recreations". These two went on many expeditions, together or with others, on their free days, often to the Forest of Dean. About a certain occasion, Frederick wrote, "On a walk of 20 to 30 miles, in particular

I remember our noting of flowers and butterflies, our scrambles up cliffs, swims in the Wye, visiting of old ruins and older moot and rocking stones. What a wonderful amount of information he, as senior member of our party poured into our ears. Then sitting together at the window, overlooking the horseshoe bend of the Severn, and with the smell of new-mown hay in our nostrils, he enlarged to those who had not been with us, on the events of the excursion. He was, as ever, at this time, full of fun and apt illustration. Nothing was wrongly stated - nothing was not strictly true - and yet we had not seen with his eyes until now .... His power of story-telling was something extraordinary."

It seemed that when John arrived in Gloucester, he was not, as one of his friends said "much of a religious professor". However, he experienced a religious crisis, when, as he, himself put it "my take-it-easy Quakerism went to pieces in the storm". He toyed with the idea of becoming an Anglican but decided that, instead, he would begin to read Quaker literature. He read Barclay's *Apology* and found himself sympathetic to the writings of more mystical Friends. Isaac Penington was the one writer who especially influenced him. One effect on him was to give up smoking, which he did in a dramatic manner by throwing all his smoking gear out of a train window when returning from an expedition. Moreover, he started to use the old Quaker form of address of "Thee" and "Thou", and adopted Quaker dress (a brown collarless coat and a broad-brimmed hat) at a time when most Friends had discarded it. Fortunately for him, his charm of manner enabled him to get away with these idiosyncrasies.

His friends found his behaviour somewhat odd. They tried to stop him from working day and night for his employer and were concerned when he forwent their companionship on their country outings. However, they respected his decisions, regarding them as being difficult but sincere. For John, Quakerism became the bedrock of his life. He seldom spoke of his beliefs but they are apparent in his letters to friends, especially to those who, going through difficult times, sought his advice. Frederick and John remained in friendship until John's death despite some fundamental differences between them.

In 1858, his employer, Mr. Wait, returning from a visit to Bristol, suddenly suggested that John should set up his own business, taking on the printing orders from the grocery trade at agreed rates. Reluctantly, John agreed; found premises in Commercial Road and installed suitable machinery. Within a week of starting, Mr. Wait reneged on his agreement. It was too late for John to change his mind, but without even the promised work, he decided to go ahead. It was chiefly due to the advice and assistance of Samuel Bowly that this step was taken. He employed a boy only and, working himself sometimes all night, he gradually established his business. His workforce increased and he was able to introduce a Steam Press, the first in Gloucester. He, himself, lived above the workshop where there was room to give his ageing parents a home. As the business grew, more space was needed for his presses so the three of them moved to Albion Cottage.

Five years later he was lucky enough to be asked by the executors of Edward Power, the leading printer in the city, to purchase his business on easy terms of payment. He now moved to 6 Westgate Street and despite the debts already incurred by his initial capital outlay, and this additional financial burden, his business prospered and he was soon cleared of his liabilities.

CHAPTER III

A Winter Journey and The Dictionary

SHORTLY BEFORE HIS MOVE to the new premises in Westgate Street, John went on an unexpected journey. This is described in a book which he wrote some four years later *A Winter Journey from Gloucester to Norway* published by Trübner. The purpose of his travels are not explained in the book, and it seems surprising that he should have left his small business at a vital time, before he knew of the plans of Edward Power's trustees.

John had been in the habit of distributing Bibles to sailors in the Gloucester Docks where many ships from Norway berthed, bringing timber for the flourishing match trade. He became particularly friendly with a Norwegian sea-captain's daughter, whom he came to love and intended to marry. When he heard that she was seriously ill, he immediately set out for her home. He describes his journey thus,

"In the beginning of 1863, and while it was yet winter, I had to go on a flying visit to Arendal, on the southern coast of Norway. Circumstances, beyond my control, permitted no choice as to the season, which rendered travelling extremely difficult; the usual means of conveyance being suspended until Spring. I was furthermore restricted as to time; and having to leave a business requiring close attention, it was desirable to make my absence from it as brief as possible .... my portmanteau was packed up without further delay; and with twenty-five pounds in my pocket, a great-coat on my back, and a railway rug on my arm, I sallied forth at midnight to take the mail train for London. I took with me some books and newspapers in Norsk, with which to practise the language as much as possible, in the day or two that intervened, before I should be thrown upon my own resources for speaking it; and I had already

10

picked up a few words and phrases from Norwegian seamen in our own Docks during the previous year or two, little supposing I might ever have such an occasion to use them".

The first part of his journey was tiresomely slow, but not too eventful. He travelled to Hamburg, thence to Copenhagen and Helsingburg in Sweden. Wherever he went, he met with helpfulness from his fellow travellers (occasionally to an oppressive degree). The overland journey to Gothenburg, by horse-drawn vehicles of various kinds, became frustratingly prolonged but also hazardous. He was lucky to meet a friendly Swedish Quartermaster, Carl Schonbeck, who had served in the Crimea; he offered John company and lodging when they reached Engelholm.

"We stopped at the door of a comfortable house; and my friend led the way through a court-yard to a warm apartment, where a motherly old lady received me with a smile of welcome that at once made me at home. Fresh logs were put into the stove - a great pillar of three or four feet in diameter reaching up to the ceiling, and covered with glazed tiles. Tea was brought in, and the luxury of its warmth was more than can be easily described .... The cold was now intense. I felt it piercing through my coat and rug as though they had been but sheets of paper, and got in doors with my teeth chattering and my nose blue from its effects. The old lady "overhauled" my great-coat, tightened the buttons with a needle and thread, and put me in sailing trim for the morning. It was now pouring with rain and sleet. I got wet and bitterly cold, and was scarcely able to dismount from the wretched "donkey carts" as I arrived at each station. The monotony of the ride was broken now and then by crossing some splendid stream or stopping at a toll-bar; and it was not a little amusing to send into one of these houses a coin, like an English penny, and receive back several smaller ones in exchange."

So he journeyed from station to station, changing from one vehicle to another, with fresh horses at each stage, travelling many miles of appalling roads to Gothenburg.

Here he had the good fortune to meet a Norwegian Captain Kröger with his son, Jan, who were also bound for Arendal. No boats were yet running regularly up the coast, but, with the help of the Captain, John was able to arrange a passage to Stromstäd on a herring boat. "A most discouraging sight presented itself, when we got on board the boat. The deck was frozen like glass, and rime frost stood on the cordage and sail; there was no fire, nor indeed any place to make one, except a small contrivance for boiling a kettle in the cabin forward. This cabin was big enough to hold four people, sitting two on each side, with their heads just low enough to escape being kicked by the mariners or passengers on deck. There was a hold, to be sure; but it would not "hold" much. They had put into it sundry casks of fish, and the like, and I placed my hat on one of these for security. It was an unlucky thought, however, for it got trodden on once or twice during the day; and I sat on it myself in the gloom of the evening, in mistake for a barrel-head, whereby it was flattened out into a disc, which it required much time and the application of sea water to restore to an approximation of its original form."

From Strömstad, a smaller boat took them across the Christiania Fjord,but then bad weather forced them to land at the small off-shore island of Kjömöe, where

"A single house stood there, under a wood of fir trees, and one or two ships were at anchor near the shore...... We landed within a yard or two of the dwelling, and went up to it to ask for a lodging....... We were welcomed by a kind-looking man, somewhat past the prime of life, who assured us he would do the best he could to make us comfortable. On entering the little parlour I could not help running up to the iron stove and clasping it round, being well-nigh frozen with cold. The host made some remark to Captain Kröger about my appearing to suffer much from it, and I heard the latter say in a low tone "Han er Engelskman, og Landmand!" (He is an Englishman, and a landsman!) Whereupon the host said to me in good clear English, "And so you come from England, sir? May I ask where you live there?"

"At Gloucester," I replied.

"Indeed! then perhaps you recollect me, for I was at your house two years ago! My name is J———, captain of the ———. How are your father and mother?"

I need not say how much this took me by surprise. Here we were, driven out of our track by stress of weather, and compelled to land at a strange spot to beg shelter for the night; and yet in this very place, where I first touched Norwegian soil, I had the pleasure of meeting with an old friend."

12

When once again on the mainland, John travelled as fast as the dreadful roads and bad weather allowed and, eventually, arrived in Arendal at midnight. He put up in an hotel and, the following day, he was directed to Captain H's home...... "Captain H—— came out and seized me by the hand, and instantly drew me into his house, where I received such kindness as I can never forget." To John's great distress, the Captain told him that his daughter had died a few days before John's arrival.

His sad return to England was, relatively speedy, as by now, he could travel by sea. He boarded a ship at Christiansand and travelled by sea and rail to Brussels where he stayed with his brother, Forster, thereafter returning to England. The account ends thus, "And now it is no more: its aeons of hopes and fears is swept into the past — and — *sic transit gloria mundi*!"

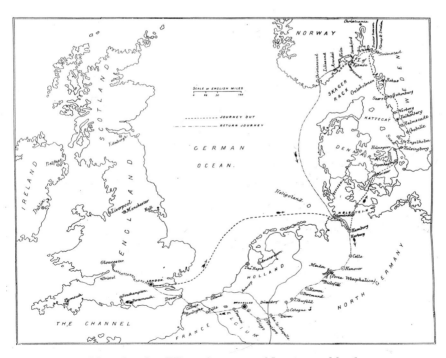

Map showing Winter journey to Norway and back

It is clear, from *A Winter Journey*, that John knew surprisingly little French or German - he mentions "ignorance of German" and writes of a "German who could speak French, but I could not." However, he quickly added to the smattering of Norwegian he had picked up from seamen in the Gloucester Docks and, evidently had a natural facility for languages.

The only Norwegian dictionary available at the time of his visit to Norway was a bulky, two-volume affair which John found irritating when he had to "unpack a portmanteau for the sake of a word." This frustration led him to envisage a small volume which could actually be carried in a traveller's pocket. He decided that French would be in greater demand, being more widely used than Norwegian.

As a young man he had mastered Cornish well enough to engage on compiling a Cornish dictionary, but before he had completed it, a standard work came on to the market. Nevertheless, his love of all things Cornish had, in the 1860's, led him to take an interest in Cornish place names, and, through this, he was in correspondence with Max Müller, Oxford Professor of Philology. In the earliest recorded letter, dated September 1866, he wrote,

"The etymology of names and places is in a very loose state in the county (Cornwall). The people are almost as quick as the Irish are at coining reason, when they have none at hand. For instance, the old Cornish name for Falmouth was, they say, Penny-come-quick; and they tell a most improbable story to account for it. I believe the whole compound is only a sort of English or 'Saxon' pun upon *Pen y cwm gwic*, Head of the creek valley. In like manner they have turned *Bryn Whella*, 'Highest Hill' into Brown Willy, and *Cwm ta goed*, Woodhouse valley, into Come-to-good".

A lively exchange of letters between these two continued for several years on a broad range of subjects. In the same year, John had suggested to Max Müller that they might plan a 'skeleton dictionary' in which travellers and missionaries might record the vocabulary of any particular language or dialect they wished to study. Professor Müller compiled a key-alphabet and introduction to the book, which was published in 1867. A further edition, containing notes on writing Chinese with Roman letters, by Professor Summers, was published by John Bellows in 1868.

Meanwhile, he was already working on the French Dictionary, as well as running his printing business. He imagined that he might finish it within a year but, in the event, it was to take him 7 years! His first task was to become familiar with the French language: he read current literature, magazines and newspapers, as well as the French classics, to be conversant with modern idioms and expressions. He also needed the help of experts and he found, possibly with Max Müller's assistance, two gifted Frenchmen, the first being M. Auguste Beljame and then, after his death, his brother, Professor Alexandre Beljame. They carefully corrected and authenticated every query that he sent them. In 1870 Professor Beljame and his wife visited John at his home, and, whilst there, had news of the fall of Sedan (in the Franco-Prussian war). They left immediately, fearing that the Germans would besiege Paris. During the siege, a shell burst in the house next to their own. M. Beljame wrote "My first thought was for the safety of my wife; but my next was for the dictionary, and I immediately moved both to more secure quarters."

A contemporary, John Bassett, in describing his life at the printing works, wrote,

"It is a marvel that such accuracy has been attained, when it is taken into account that the work was prepared during office hours, and in the midst of his workmen - both compositors and machinists. Thousands of times has his attention been drawn away from the rendering of a French phrase: sometimes to write an order for "sorts", now to correct a handbill or circular, or an order for paper, or to help a compositor in the selection of a display line....... The steady perseverance of Mr. Bellows cannot be too highly commended with interruptions such as these."

John, himself, wrote, "Of the weary months of correcting I took no note; but at last I concluded I must make the best of it, and I must go on to the end, fighting my way through all disappointments till I compelled success, even if it half ruined me. I had fully steeled myself for the disappointment of seeing it left on my hands unappreciated: for with all due respect to the 'enlightened public', it is such a fickle body that absolute merit, even supposing my work to possess merit in proportion to the labour bestowed on it is not always a guarantee of success. "Your book will never sell" remarked the most far-seeing of my friends, "I have always said so; for the print is so small that no one can read it."....... Professor Blackie, of Edinburgh, however, cheered me with a different forecast. "I see by the way you set about it" he said, "that you have a dash of enthusiasm about you, and that you will go through with your book for the love of it, whether it pays you or not; but I think I can promise you, from what I see of its plan, that in twelve months from the time it is published, it will be all over the world as the best French dictionary ever printed."

John's conception of the new dictionary was wholly original. As a printer, he used his professional knowledge by depicting parts of speech in different forms of type. Each page was divided into two, with the upper half containing Français-Anglais, and the lower English-French (words). To produce a volume measuring only 4⅛ ins. x 2⅝ ins., he needed specially thin paper and small type was specially cast by Miller & Richard of Edinburgh. The type proved to be so minute that it frequently broke off when the sheets were in the press.

Professor Blackie's forecast was amply justified, though John, himself, was not convinced. His publishers, Messrs. Trübner, wanted to produce 20,000 copies for the first edition, but he demurred, fearing that he had already risked so much money that it would be wiser to print only 6,000. Within less than twelve months, in 1873, these were all sold. The dictionary was dedicated to Prince Lucien Bonaparte, who shared John's interest in philology. He had studied dialects in France, but was now acknowledged as the foremost authority on English dialects, and now had made his home in this country. On visiting John at the Printing Works, incognito, he was immediately recognised as a relative of Napoleon, who was his uncle.

The National Press was unstinting in its praise: *The Scotsman*, *The Spectator* and *The Times* all had favourable reviews. *Punch* commented "Mr. Bellows, according to *The Times* critic, has produced a French Dictionary within pocket compass so perfect that there is no pretext for the cry "Bellows to mend."

His friends, too, were lavish in their enthusiasm. Max Müller wrote "Your dictionary is quite bewitching .... Dr. Stanley told me he had dined at the French Embassy (St. Petersburg) and all the people there had talked of the French dictionary." Oliver Wendell Holmes*, a correspondent of many years, wrote, "I never saw the ideal of minute printing made palpable until I looked into this *opusculum aureum*, in which you have condensed such an amount of information." And of the second edition, "I have been reading one of Zola's not particularly immoral but forcibly realistic stories. It has a great number of French slang words in it...... Now I found that your little microscopic dictionary was equal to the hard task I put upon it...... surprising me by the richness of its little columns and the exceedingly knowing way in which common colloquialisms were rendered into corresponding English ones...... I consider the little lexicon the very gem of my library."

One would think that John would have been satisfied with such praise, but there were aspects of the book that failed to satisfy his perfectionism. It must have been difficult for his family and friends to accept that, rather than produce further imprints of the first edition, and get rid of his debts in one fell swoop, he insisted on scrapping the original print, and, three and a half years later, produced an entirely new second edition. For this, he ordered an even finer textured paper than before and nearly ran himself into a lawsuit because thrice he refused to accept paper that was not up to his own standard. The revised second edition was reset in slightly larger type, and has been revised and re-printed some thirty times since then. As with the first edition, John Silbree M.A. of London University read and corrected the proofs, a very tedious job with such small print.

Mark Twain gave a free advertisement for the book in one of his stories, *The Church of the Gratis Lesson,* in which he described a scene in a Paris Church where a very devout congregation was following the Service in French. As he drew nearer, he found that, far from using Prayer books, the faithful were studying copies of Bellows' French dictionary! They proved to be a party of American tourists learning French on a free basis.

---

* Professor of Anatomy, at Harvard: author of *The Autocrat of the Breakfast Table* and regular contributor to *The Atlantic Monthly.*

: roger

WAX, cire [va/cirer [vz) devenir | To get in a — 1847 A
[fam] s'emporter | Sealing — Cire à cacheter | Shoemaker's —, [pers] V. WAX]
Poix | — END, — fil poissé ————

—LIGHT, bougie | —TAPER, [a é] rat de cave [to burn a
before altar) cierge | Wax'en a ... de cire | WAXING, cirage
WAX'WORKS, collection de figures de cire | Waxy a. cire

WAY [on pr oué] [road &) chemin ; route [Which is the — to ... ?
Quel est le C. de [or pour] ?] On one's — to,., En route
pour : en allant à | Over the —, En face | This right, the
— way —, Le bon, le mauvais C | The public —, La voie publique
Permanent —, voie | The — land —, de terre
To lose one's —, s'égarer | rencontre — voie dans
(figuratively) voie | The — of the Lord, Les Vs du Seigneur
To make one's — in the world, Ne Faire son chemin
To do —

[distance) distance | A long —, a great — off, Loin
This get some on her — Nous avons
de terre

[direction, whence, whither) côté | Which — ? Par où ...? D'où
Which — is the wind ? D'où vient le vent ? | I don't know
which — to turn. Je ne sais pas de quel côté
This —, That —, Par ici, par là : de ce côté-ci (or là]
—IN, entrée | — OUT, Sortie | [V. make below]
—THROUGH, passage (au travers &]
(en longueur (to, de] (from, de]

[direction & placing, &c.&) sens | The long —, Dans le sens de la
longueur | The wrong —, à travers [against the grain &) à rebours
The wrong — up, Sens dessus dessous.

[means) moyen | the, An easy way of getting a living, M. facile de
gagner sa vie | There's no — of managing it, Il n'y a pas de moyen
Is there any — of getting ... on to Nantes tonight?

[mode of doing &). manière | In this —, De cette M, In some — or
other, D'une façon ou d'autre | In the English —, German —,
à l'anglaise; à l'allemande | Is this the — to ? Est ainsi
qu'on ...?] The right, — La bonne, mauvaise
manière [a) comme il faut | The wrong —, mal La mauvaise
M [ad) mal | To get into the — of it, l'idée | To do a —,
Faire ... à ma manière | To put) in a —, mettre sur la voie de ...

[way of acting &) manière | It's his — C'est sa M | Children's little

Words common to both languages are given in the French division only.

WAT ENGLISH—FRENCH WAY
W comme OU dans le mot OUI. ✷ A comme O dans **SORT**.

✷ **Wa'ter** va. arroser [give ... to drink] abreuver [silks, etc.) moirer [one's wine, etc.] couper : mettre de l'*eau* dans : 'baptiser' [*vn.*) pleurer [take in _) faire de l'*eau* | It makes one's mouth _, Cela fait venir l'*eau à la bouche*

✷ **WA'TERFALL** *cascade* [larger) *chute* d'*eau*

✷ **WA'TER-HEN** *poule* d'*eau*

✷ **WA'TERING** [of land) *irrigation* [of streets) arrosement [of plants, &c.) arrosage [of wines, fraud) mouillage [of silks, etc.) moirage [letting ... drink) abreuvage [taking in water) approvisionnement d'*eau* | _ PLACE [for cattle) abreuvoir [sea-side town) *plage* [for an inland town, such as Vichy) *eaux* (pl] *ville* d'*eaux* | -POT arrosoir

✷ **WA'TERMAN** [*me-nn*] [pl. _men] batelier [for cab horses) servant de *place*

✷ **WA'TERPLANE** hydravion

✷ **WA'TERPROOF** imperméable [a *lady's* _) 'waterproof' [*a.*) imperméable [*va.*) rendre imperméable : imperméabiliser

✷ **WA'TERSHED** versant | Line of the _, *Ligne* de partage *des eaux* | *crête* de P

✷ **WA'TERSPOUT** [*spaoûtt*] trombe

✷ **WA'TERWORKS** (pl] *eaux : installation des eaux* : réservoir

✷ **Wa'tery** a. aqueux [poet) liquide

✷ **WAT'TLE** clayonnage [tree) acacia

✷ **WAT'TLES** (pl] barbe

✷ **Wat'tle'd** a. lié avec de l'osier

WAVE [*ouéve*] *vague : lame : ondulation : flot* [of the hand, etc.) signe [poet) onde | Light _, *Onde lumineuse* | Sound _, *O sonore* — *vn.* flotter : s'agiter [*va.*) a handkerchief, etc.) agiter [one's hand) faire signe (de *la main*) [the hair) onduler | _ RULE [typ] filet

Wa'ver [a *é*] *vn.* hésiter : vaciller [trembler

WA'VERING [a *é*] *hésitation : vacillation* — *a.* vacillant : inconstant : irrésolu

WA'VINESS [a, *é*] état ondulé : *ondulation*

Wa'vy [*oué'-vé*] a. ondoyant

WAX *cire* [*va.*) cirer [*vn.*) devenir | To get in a _ [fam] 'Rager' | Sealing _, *Cire à cacheter* | Shoemaker's _, *Poix* | -END fil poissé [shoemakers call it ligneul] -LIG'HT *bougie* | _ MATCH *allumette-bougie* | TA'PER [a *é*] rat de *cave* [to burn before altar) cierge

Wax'e'n a. ... de *cire*

WAX'ING cirage

WAX'WING jaseur (de *Bohême*)

WAX'WORK | Like _, [fig] Fait au tour _S (pl] *collection* de *figures* de *cire : galerie* de groupes en *cire*

Wax'y a. en *cire* : ciré [pers., *V.* Wax]

WAY [*oué*] (road) chemin : *route* [fig., as _ of the Lord, etc.) *voie* [*ship's* speed, *V. ERRE*] [of saws) *chasse* | Which is the _ to ...? Quel est le chemin de [or *pour* aller à] ...? | On one's _ to ..., En *route* pour ... : allant à | I was on my _ back to, Je rentrais à | I was on my _ back from, Je revenais de ... [*V.* Other : Out] Over the _, En *face* | The right, the wrong _, Le bon, le mauvais chemin | The public _, *La voie publique* | The permanent _, [🚂] *La voie* | The land _, [*ad.*] *La voie de terre* | To lose one's _, S'égarer : se perdre | To stop the _, Barrer le passage | _ IN *entrée* (to, de] _ OUT *sortie* (from,

de] _ THROUGH *passage* (au travers, etc.] [*V.* Make, 1st column, p. 670] If it comes in my _, Si je le [or *la*] rencontre | ... by a long _, à beaucoup près | RIGHT of _, Droit de passage

[distance) *distance* | A long _, a great _ off, Loin : très loin [*V.* Great, Little _, in the first column on next page]

[direction, whence, whither) côté | Which _? Par où ...? D'où ...? | Which _ is the WIND? D'où vient le vent? | I don't know which _ to turn, Je ne sais de quel côté aller | This _, that _, Par ici, par là : de ce côté-ci [or -là]

[direction of placing, etc.) sens | The long _, [*ad.*] Dans le sens de *la longueur* [or, en long] The wrong _, Dans le mauvais sens : de travers [against the grain, etc.) à rebours : à rebrousse-poil | The wrong _ up, Sens dessus dessous

[means) moyen | An easy _ of getting a living, Un moyen facile de gagner *sa vie* | There's no _ of managing it, Il n'y a pas moyen : 'il n'y a pas *mèche*' | Is there any _ of getting on to Nantes to-night? Y a-t-il moyen d'arriver à Nantes ce soir?

[manner) *manière* | In this _, De *cette M* | In some _ or other, D'*une façon* ou d'*une autre* | In such a _ that, De *telle sorte* que | In the English _, German _, à *l'anglaise*, à *l'allemande* | Is this the _ to speak? Est-ce ainsi qu'on parle? | The *right* _, *La bonne M* [*ad.*] comme il faut | The wrong _, *La mauvaise M* [*ad.*] mal | I tried him every _, Je l'ai pris de *toutes les façons* | To get into the _ of it, S'y mettre | I do it my' _, J'en fais à *ma tête* : je le fais à *mon idée* | To put ... in a _ to ..., Mettre ... en *voie de* ...

[way of acting, etc.) *manière* | It's his _, C'est *sa manière* de faire | He's going on in his old _, Il va toujours son train | Children's little _s, Les *petites roueries* des enfants | Pretty _s, *Gentillesses* | He has a _ of, (a trick of] Il a *une certaine manière de* ... | It is just the _ with such people, to ...! La *manière* d'agir de ces gens-là, c'est de ...! | It is the _ of the WORLD! Ainsi va le monde! | In a friendly _, En ami | In a plain _, Simplement [fam] 'à *la bonne franquette*' | The better _ would be to ..., Le mieux serait de ...

[state, condition) état | In a fair _ to ..., En train de ... : en *passe de* : en *voie de* | He's in a sad _ about it! Il en est tout démonté!

[line of business, etc.) *partie* : métier | Not in his _, Pas de *sa partie* [or de son ressort] What _ is he in? Que fait-il? | He's in a large _, Il fait *des affaires* en grand | In a business _, Comme en *affaires* | In the _, En fait de livres

[own will, etc.) He has his own _, He will have his _, Il en fait à *sa tête*

[sense) sens | In this _, Comment dois-je entendre ceci? | Better in every _, Mieux de *toutes les façons*

By _ of, [instead of : for the purpose of] à titre de | By _ of remembering it, *Pour* ne pas l'oublier [See next page

CHAPTER IV

Marriage and *The Track of the War around Metz*

ONCE JOHN HAD DECIDED to work on the dictionary, the next seven or eight years were extremely busy ones. It was during this time that he met Elizabeth Earnshaw. On New Year's Day, 1868, by reason of a change in the Factory Act, his Printing Works came under its jurisdiction and, in consequence, the Steam Press received a visit from the local Factory Inspector, Hugh Earnshaw. He and John formed an immediate friendship and, in due course, John was invited to spend a night at Hugh's house in Minchinhampton. There he met Elizabeth, who had come down from her home in Clitheroe, Lancashire, to stay with her brother.

Elizabeth Earnshaw 1862

Perhaps this encounter made John realise that his present accommodation was far from ideal. Early in the spring of the same year, he found Handlow

20

HANDLOW HOUSE
·CHURCHAM·

Handlow House, Churcham, near Gloucester

House in Churcham, a village a few miles west of Gloucester. It was an attractive, small building, with a garden, and surrounded by fields; wonderfully quiet compared with the turmoil of Westgate Street.

He moved there with his parents: William, who was now seventy years old and Hannah, in increasingly poor health. She had suffered from some kind of rheumatic disease most of her life and was, at one time, confined to her bed for two years.

It was said that here, in the garden of Handlow House, John proposed to Elizabeth and was accepted. With a nice, romantic touch, he picked her a bunch of purple violets and asked what she would most like for her first wedding present. She suggested a tea-set, which, later on, he gave her - one decorated with violets, two plates of the set still survive! Throughout their lives, both he and Elizabeth derived much pleasure from their garden. She had a

John Bellows in the late 1860's

special interest in campanulas: as for him, a photograph shows him weeding the lawn on bended knees and wearing his top-hat. Perhaps he wore one when he proposed to her in the garden.

In January 1869 they were married in Clitheroe where Elizabeth's father Mark Earnshaw, practised as a surgeon. Elizabeth was the fifth child in a family of six; their home, 2 York Street, in the middle of the town, was still standing in 1982. It retained a surprisingly rural outlook at the rear, with an uninterrupted view of a steep, grassy hillside.

In an obituary in *The Friend* , Elizabeth was described as "having a character of intermingling strength and tenderness", and these qualities must have stood her in good stead for the varied and strenuous life that lay ahead. Their first child, Max, named after Max Müller, was born in 1870, and was only 5 months old when his father felt called to spend a month in Metz during the Franco-Prussian War, for the Quaker War Victims' Fund. What we know of this period and, indeed, of much of his life, comes to us through his correspondence with his friends and his wife. The letters to her reveal how much they shared, even when they were apart. It may seem strange, for example, that he should have left his new wife, with a baby and his two elderly parents to look after, and go into the war zone, but it is probable that Elizabeth, too, shared his convictions and was prepared to accept such a challenge, though personal matters were, naturally, edited out of his letters when he published them as *The Track of the War around Metz* on his return home.

His month in France is best described by himself: he first explains how members of The Society of Friends were much concerned with the plight of the peasants in an area of France over-run by German soldiers. "First, they had to ascertain to what extent this suffering had spread...... To do this, five young men were despatched to the seat of war, who made rapid journeys on horseback over the ravaged districts, and brought home particulars of the state of things they found there...... The Friends, being a small body .... made a general appeal. It has been well responded to." The Society decided that the administration of this fund should be accomplished by a volunteer service. He then explains that the volunteers called "Commissioners" should either fund themselves or

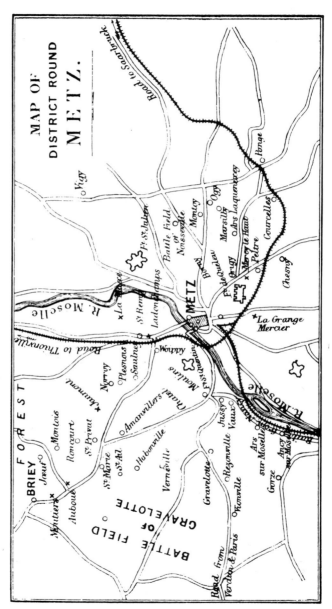

Map of Metz

24

if unable to do so, have all their expenses paid through a separate fund. Thus, all the money collected publicly would be spent on food and clothing for the suffering peasants.

"Hence it happened that the present writer was asked to take his turn with others; and I accordingly started for Metz about four weeks after Bazaine's surrender of that city (end of Nov. 1870) .....
I carried a sheet of paper in my hat, and whenever there was a spare moment, I took it out and wrote - sometimes at breakfast, and in the middle of carrying on a conversation; sometimes at our stores, with all sorts of stir and bustle .... and still oftener in the small hours of the night when I ought to have been in bed and asleep."

His first letter is from Brussels and is dated 27 November 1870: it describes his journey so far. He was helped by the Station-master at Dover, who recommended that he travel via Lille,

"but I told him I had promised my wife to go as little as possible into France, and would therefore take an Ostend ticket ..... T. Newman (a Friend) pasted two of the large star labels on my portmanteaus. This has done me good service, for the custom-house officers have never asked me to open either, but hand them over intact."

This was the first time that the black and red star was used; the English Minister in Brussels advised such usage, in lieu of the Red Cross, which had been abused and worn by unauthorised citizens. John Bellows found the star respected throughout his travels in Prussia and around Metz. In addition, he carried a "Commission", a document of identity and Christian purpose in French and German.

Two days later, travelling via Luxembourg and, circuitously, touching on Trèves and Saarbrück, he reached Metz. On the first day, he was overseeing the unloading of potatoes from Luxembourg by four French National Guards.

"Whilst four Prussian sentinels marched to and fro near us, with bayonets fixed, to keep anyone from interfering with the train who had no right to .... The Prussians, I need not say, throng many parts of the town, but every hour some of them leave for Nancy or Paris....... But a word about our lodgings. On my arrival at the hotel, I found that four Friends were at Metz, or in the district.

25

They have far more work than they can keep up with, as thou may'st fancy when I say sixty villages require inspection, and many of them regular relief. Curés, Maires, and all sorts of people, write or come to us every day to make arrangements for food, etc. etc.."

Most of his days were spent in visiting villages and assessing their needs: sometimes on foot or in one of the wagons, occasionally on horseback. He visited Briey one day with two wagons, and on reaching the Hôtel de Ville, found the Maire was much distressed, having just received documents requisitioning food, so that anything that they had brought would be taken. So John decided to postpone the delivery. "I had some further talk with them about seeds etc; and trust the committee will help them in this way in the Spring.

It was nearly 7 o'clock when everything was arranged...... I left the horse to be brought on to St. Privat next day with the carts, and as it was bright moonlight, I started to walk alone to this village, which might be eight miles off. The valley was very beautiful and it was a relief to be by myself." But he was tired at the end of the day,

St Privat. A war-ruined house (drawing by J.B.)

and hailed a covered wagon, driven by German soldiers. "They instantly pulled up, and I clambered in amongst them, stumbling over knapsacks and needle guns...... I got down at Ste. Marie au Chênes, and called on the Curé...... He dragged me in with a warm grasp of the hand, and insisted that I should go no further that night...... The Curé told me of the coming up of the innumerable hosts of men on the morning after the battle and the terror of the poor villagers, who all, three hundred in number, flocked to his house as to a common refuge." (The Curé was describing the Battle of Gravelotte, where some forty thousand German and French were said to have been killed or wounded, the Germans called Ste. Marie aux Chênes "The grave of the Guards")...... "At first, he could hardly stand against the shivering of horror that passed through him at such sights; but being gifted with strong health and energy, he got over this and laboured all day long, from early morning till far into the night for six whole weeks, among the dying and the dead."

His experiences with Germans was very varied: at Auboue, the whole village had been ransacked by the Prussians. They had seized everything from the house of the Maire,

"even dragging the bed clothes off and taking them away. The furniture was smashed and all the earthenware, except a few plates, clear gone." He was, again, unable to leave stores because of expected requisitioning. "So I sent on the wagons (an empty one followed by the one with the bread) and my horse; I following on foot." Two roads led to Briey, "The place is exceedingly like the road below the hill at Brinscombe...... I had scarcely got to the top of the plateau, when I saw the head of a column of infantry emerging from a wooded bend..... There were our two wagons, with the horse slowly trailing along at the tail of the hindmost, and it occurred to me that, if the Prussians saw him riderless, they would "requisition" him there and then. Quick as a lamplighter, I ran and jumped down the slope, at the no small hazard of going head over heels, to get to the horse before the soldiers came up. They were amused at the scene, for they jested me in German as they filed past; but I was already on the horse, and "all right".

Yet these "conquering Germans ..... sit down by the side of the people they are quartered upon, and weep with them very bitter tears ..... and tell with touching simplicity of their wives and little ones, whom they will probably never see again! *They will stand in a line* to take turns to clasp a little baby in their arms and kiss it."

Constantly he was struck by the contrast between the beauty of the countryside and the desolate areas of battlefields.

"Away on either hand, stretched the plain; behind, and far off, was the valley of the beautiful Moselle, and the blue hills of the Vosges (?) - and before, at an immense distance, other blue hills. It was not long before I reached St. Privat. Ah, what a sight! Up on this bleak and desolate plain, there seemed to be ploughed land; as I drew nearer I found it was trampled by thousands of footmarks, and furrowed deep by wheels of cannon. Something shining on the ground attracted me; I saw it was a bayonet - and a man passing at the moment, I gave him a couple of sous to fetch it to me as I sat on my horse. It began to snow; the ground was frozen hard, and I rode into the village. A row of black staring ruins, roofless, windowless and doorless, met my view."

The Commissioners were aware that, as well as supplying the immediate necessities of life to the French smallholders and farmers, it was essential that they brought their land back into cultivation. John wrote,

"I attended a meeting of the Chamber of Agriculture of the arrondissement, to ask the members about our sending out a steam plough..... the chamber accepts our offer .... and we are now engaged in getting up a number of necessary details for their despatch and working."

In addition, they needed seed corn and seed potatoes, and, on December 21st, just before leaving Metz, John wrote to *The Times*, asking for the help of English farmers, both for seeds and money. The letter was published in full on December 24th and included the Metz Chamber of Agriculture's suggestion that the recipients were to be divided into three categories: those who could pay in full, those who could make a contribution and those without any resources. John added that "small assortments for the cottagers, such as beans, peas, carrots and salad herbs, which the French cook up in a variety of ways that an Englishman would never dream of" should be included. He also mentioned the type of soil around

28

Briey, the worst affected area, and that a depot in London would be made available for storage of the goods donated. Other practical details were noted.

This letter, and a further letter to *The Times*, published on January 21st 1871, and signed by himself and Arthur Albright, as Hon. Secretaries of The Society of Friends Seed Corn Committee, must have contributed to the large quantity of seeds that were eventually distributed for Spring sowing (28,000 bushels of barley, oats and other grains, and 970 tons of seed potatoes - steeped, to render them inedible).

By now, John's time in Metz was nearly over: he records one incident which he felt drew discredit on himself and one or two of his colleagues who, like him, had collected a few curiosities, among them being weapons (a bayonet has already been mentioned). The Prussians got wind of this and the Friends premises were searched, resulting in the confiscation of all their "relics". One of their group was seized and spent two days in prison before explanations were accepted. His release was due, mainly, to the support given them by the Préfet, who knew them well. They were very lucky for they had committed an offence against military law.

When John first arrived in Metz, the city, which had only recently surrendered after the siege, was in the throes of a typhus epidemic. Three hundred and fifty railway carriages were assembled in the main square and used as a temporary fever hospital. Of the Friends with whom John worked, none had caught typhus, but eight had been ill and five of these contracted smallpox, though the others remained reasonably fit. The Allen family of Dublin suffered most: Henry Allen had been the first to succumb to smallpox, and his sister, Ellen and his Uncle Richard came to Metz to nurse him. Both caught the disease, and Ellen became gravely ill. On the very morning that John was due to go home and was already at the station, Thomas Whitwell, also homeward bound, brought the news that Ellen was dying. They rushed back, but she had already died before they reached her.

This tragic conclusion to their courageous work on behalf of the victims of the war was, indeed, hard to bear, but it is certain that not one of them would ever regret their endeavours.

CHAPTER V

Peace, Printing and Pamphlets

WHEN JOHN RETURNED to Gloucester he was asked to become Secretary of the Metz Seed Corn Committee, and, thereby, was able to follow the progress of the relief efforts until April when Friends finally left Metz.

John published his *Track of the War around Metz* in 1871 (Trübner, London). In the concluding paragraph, he showed forcibly that he did not deceive himself into "believing that he had been engaged in a particularly religious work". He wrote,

"so far indeed, is the busy "philanthropic" working which is now so popular, from being a necessary accompaniment to a healthy religious life ...... that it is .... secretly, yet unmistakedly leaned on as an easy means of compromising for the neglect of closer and weightier duty."

He was profoundly influenced by his experiences in the battle areas and this forced him to review his own position as a pacifist. It seems that Max Müller had written to him, asking for his views and he responded in a letter (Feb. 1871). "I candidly admit I don't know how to answer thy question. What would I do if my wife and child lived in Saarbrück and the French were to come and bombard the town? I run, mentally, in a moment, over the line of argument that suggests itself, and find myself at the other end of that line - *bombarding the French*. But, what French? Those who came to Saarbrück or others who had nothing to do with that? People call war justice on a large scale; but the mischief is that it is only the vastness of the scale that prevents our seeing there is no justice about it".

He wrote of his sympathy for the soldiers and what they suffer, and of the terrible injustices and hardships caused by war, involving the civilian population.

"I am aware my letter is still no answer to thy question. The really Christian standard makes no provision whatever for such contingencies..... The peace principle it seems to me depends on the spiritual state of the individual, as to its being carried out; not all on mere opinions, whether "Quaker" or political, but on the degree of a man's growth into, and acting from, the Divine nature itself. P.S. My little Max flourishes like a green bay tree: but he is by no means as still as that plant."

Elizabeth must have been vastly relieved to have John back again, and to share with him the changes in young Max, now 6 months old. John's letters from the war zone with his graphic descriptions of the horrors he encountered must have often frightened her.

In March, Oliver Wendell Holmes wrote, "I have received your little book *The Track of the War around Metz* and have just been reading it through from beginning to end. It has interested me very much, and inspired me with new respect for a Christian body which sends forth such missionaries of humanity to the suffering multitudes of a nation alien in race and language, but one with them as children of the common Father.

Your simple narrative of what you did and what you saw is worth many a showy volume in which the writer has told, for the sake of reputation, of the sights he visited from no higher motive than curiosity. I see my wife at this moment deep in its pages, and I am sure it will find sympathising readers wherever there are good men and women."

In the following year, 1872, the lease on the Westgate Street premises was due to expire, and John had to face the fact that he had to move, and at the same time to provide larger premises for his expanding business. He therefore purchased Eastgate House, a property in the centre of the city, which had a fairly large garden. He planned to build the new printing works and offices on the garden site, and, whilst the workmen were digging the foundations, they came across a mass of masonry, coins and other objects which

Gloucester Printing Works 1882

Gloucester Printing Works 1920s/1930s

John recognised as probably Roman in origin*. His interest in archaeology was re-kindled by this discovery, and led him to further finds.

The family moved into Eastgate House in September 1873 - now with 3 children - Marian and baby Willie as well as Max. There was sadness at leaving Handlow House and the countryside, and sadness, too, when, shortly after they had moved, John's mother, Hannah, died. During her last illness, he wrote to Max Müller.

"Life is full of sorrows and troubles, and I have had some heavy ones; but I don't know how to steel myself against the blow that I dread may soon fall on us in parting with my mother. The cares of business and of little children ought to harden one into manhood at two and forty; but when I think of my mother I come back to be a little child again myself. I think thou will *feel* what I mean, but I can't write more."

Four years later, he wrote to an Edinburgh friend, Bruce Home,

"I buried my father yesterday. He was ready to die, and met Death as patiently and cheerfully as he would have prepared for a change of abode in this world, had it been his lot."

As a printer John had an excellent reputation for careful and accurate work (which he had put to good use on his own behalf in the printing of his Dictionary). But he insisted that no work should be taken on that was, in its nature, contrary to his own personal convictions. He refused all programmes for music and theatre: he went so far as to refuse items dealing with temperance or Adult-School gatherings if there was the slightest allusion to singing or instrumental music. The people of Gloucester found this hard indeed to understand: they were more sympathetic to his refusal of brewers or wine merchants' material as he was a known teetotaller. When an order went out with an offending line which had escaped his notice, he charged only the cost price.

Despite these scruples, his business flourished and the premises in Eastgate continued with an expanding workforce. When he died, in 1902, he was employing about a hundred workers; two of these,

---

* The importance of finding this, the first piece of Roman Wall in Gloucester, and other relics is described by Malcolm Watkins, Archaelogical Director of Gloucester Museum, on page 113.

Bellows' Rapid Wages Cylinder

FOR PAYMENT OF DAY-WORK ON THE NINE HOURS' SCALE, OR PAYMENT BY THE HOUR

Price 80/.

COPYRIGHT—JOHN BELLOWS, GLOUCESTER

THIS instrument consists of a drum containing from 40 to 50 columns of figures representing rates of wages per week, per day, per hour, as the case may be. In front, and nearly in the position of the rest of a lathe for wood-turning, is a fixed bar, on which are marked, in bold figures, the rates themselves; each rate, of course, standing opposite the column on the cylinder containing the calculations for that rate; say, for a "weekly" pay, from 1 hour up to 80. The hours are shown in a bold column in the centre, and by a touch of the hand upon a wheel at the end, any given hour is brought in an instant to the reading-bar, when a glance *along* the latter to the *rate* column shows the exact sum to be paid. Rates below 20/- a week stand on the *left* of the hours; 20/- and upwards, on the *right*

	20/	21/	22/
33	12/3. 11/11* 12/ 12/2,	12/10 12/9 12/8, 12/9	13/5. 13/2, 13/3 13/4
32	11/10 11/7 11/8 11/9	12/5. 12/2 12/3 12/4	13/. 12/9 12/10 12/11
31	11/6	12/1.	12/8.
HOURS	20/	21/	22/

Bellows' Rapid Wages Cylinder

BELLOWS' RAPID WAGES CYLINDER

Here we come to another new point. Whilst in every case the nearest *penny* is printed, no fractions (such as ¼, ½, ¾) being employed, the nearest half-penny is also shown by simply placing a dot at the top of the figure, or at the foot of it, where a half-penny *more* or a half-penny *less*, respectively, would be nearer the exact fraction due for the time indicated. The reason for discarding the usual marks ¼, ½, ¾ is two-fold. First, they are difficult to read in any small size of type; and second, the farthing and three farthings never being used in actual pay, it is but wasting the clerk's time to make him read them and then translate into another figure. For instance, as everyone would pay 9d. where 8¾d. is printed, why not print the actual 9d. at once instead of the fictitious 8¾d.?

Even where the fractions are given for the purpose of adding the quarter-hours to the hours, they are frequently misleading. For instance—the "½" may stand, and does stand, for either four tenths, five tenths, or six tenths of a penny; yet it presents no distinction to the eye, while *a penny difference ought to be made in the pay* in the latter case. Suppose a sum stands in the printed table 5/9½ it is impossible to tell from this whether we ought to *pay* 5/9 or 5/10: if the real fraction is ·6 we ought to pay 5/10: if it is ·5 *even, or less than* ·5, we ought to pay 5/9. The same remark applies to casting two farthings together in adding the quarter hours to the even hours. In a common printed table /2·3 and 10/6·3 would stand as 2¼d. and 10/6¼, so that added they only shew 10/8½—the ½ gets struck off, and the workman receives 10/8 while he *ought* to receive 10/9—and so on. My plan avoids this, by shewing in all cases *which side* of the half-penny the balance inclines.

It is not so much the value of an isolated penny or two which is worth this trouble, but the *certainty of being correct*.

RATES:—(IN ORDERING PLEASE SPECIFY WHICH SERIES IS WANTED)

No. 1 Series, 2/6 3/- 3/6 4/- 4/6 5/- 5/6 6/- 6/6 7/- 7/6 8/- 8/6 9/- 10/- 11/- 12/- and so on rising by one shilling up to 40/- but *omitting* 29/- and 39/- with 3 hour columns—one at each end and one in the centre.

No. 2 Series the same, but *including* 29/- and 39/-. In this cylinder there is only *one* hour column, in the centre, as the space taken up by the outer ones is used for the 29/- and 39/-.

No. 2b. for Manchester Engineers, with 31/6 and 40/6 instead of 30/- and 40/-.

No. 6 for use by Builders, gives rates per HOUR instead of per week, beginning at 1d. and running up to 10d. by *farthings*.

Among the Firms using these Instruments are the following:

TANGYES LIMITED, Engineers, Birmingham. (*Six*)
THE MIDLAND RAILWAY COMPANY
THE TRAFALGAR COLLIERIES, Forest of Dean
JOHN BROWN & CO., Atlas Works, Sheffield
CAMMELL & CO., Cyclops Works, Sheffield
WILSON, HAWKSWORTH, ELLISON & CO., Sheffield
CROOKES, ROBERTS & CO., Argus Works, Sheffield
W. H. PHILLIPS, BIRMINGHAM
MAY & MOUNTAIN, Birmingham
HUNTLEY & PALMERS, Reading
PEEK, FREAN & CO., London. (*Two*)
RANSOME & SIMS, Ipswich
MARSHALL, SONS & CO., Gainsborough
HIBERNIA IMPLEMENT WORKS, Dublin
BOOTH BROTHERS, Dublin
G. DUNCAN, Printer, Liverpool
HENRY HOWARD & CO., Tube Works, Dudley
BROWN & CO., Tube Works, Wednesbury
JOHN RUSSELL & CO., Tube Works, Walsall
LEWELLINS & JAMES, Brassfounders, Bristol
JOSIAH STONE & CO., Engineers & Brassfounders, Deptford
GWYNNE & CO., Essex St. Works, Strand, London
MAUDSLAY, SONS & FIELD, Engineers and Shipbuilders, London. (*Three*)
POWIS, JAMES, WESTERN & CO., Engineers, London
FOLLOWS & BATE, Engineers, Manchester
EARLE'S SHIPBUILDING COMPANY, Hull. (*Two*)
JAMES TAYLOR & CO., Engineers, Birkenhead
OSWALD & COMPANY, Shipbuilders, Sunderland
A. B. FLEMING & CO., Chemical Works, Leith
THE LANDORE SIEMENS STEEL COMPANY. (*Two*)
THE BRISTOL WAGON COMPANY
THE GLOUCESTER RAILWAY CARRIAGE & WAGON CO.
THE BIRMINGHAM WAGON COMPANY,—&c., &c.

Trafalgar Colliery, Coleford, Glo'stershire,—"We find it a very valuable assistant. Our clerks are highly delighted with it. *The Work is done with Railway speed and with more accuracy than it was before.*"

CHARLES CAMMELL & Co., Cyclops Works, Sheffield,—"Your Wages Cylinder has given us every satisfaction, and we shall be very happy to recommend it to our friends; in fact, we have done so on several occasions."

WILSON, HAWKSWORTH, ELLISON & Co., Carlisle Works, Sheffield,—"We are very much pleased with your Wages Cylinder."

TANGYES LIMITED, Cornwall Works, Birmingham, write that they save *every week* more than the year's interest on the cost of the the cylinders.

LEWELLINS & JAMES, Bristol,—"Of great value both as to accuracy and saving of time."

Engineering.—"The best we have yet seen. *It can scarcely fail to come extensively into use.*"

Bradford Daily Telegraph.—"Must be productive of an enormous saving of time and trouble in calculating workmen's wages."

Mechanic's Magazine.—"It effects a great saving of clerks' labour. Its rapidity of accuracy will establish great popularity for this invention."

English Mechanic.—"Its advantages must, we think, be patent to all who see it."

Birmingham Daily Gazette.—"So simple in its arrangement as to ensure the utmost rapidity, and so accurate in its minutest detail as to challenge the closest scrutiny."

Birmingham Daily Post.—"Something really worth seeing. *By the use of this invention the labour of wages calculation is amazingly reduced.*"

Preston Chronicle.—"**One of the most wonderful tables for calculating wages that has ever been brought before the public** . . . So arranged that to commit an error in calculating is impossible, except in case of culpable carelessness. What you want to know can be ascertained by a single glance of the eye."

Preston Herald.—Surprisingly simple yet securing unerring accuracy.

Birmingham Morning News.—"At once very ingenious and exceedingly simple, it is an instrument admirably adapted for the purpose for which it is intended. It may be fairly said, that *it surpasses everything in the nature of a wages table that has ever been produced.*"

Morning Post.—"Error is impossible." *Standard.*—"Excellent."

Chambers' Journal.—"Cannot fail to be useful where large numbers of men are employed. The clerk has only to turn the light cylinder, and in the columns of figures he sees readily the exact amount each man has to receive, according to the number of hours he may have worked."

MIDLAND RAILWAY, DERBY, August 3rd, 1872. Having given your "Rapid Wages Table" nearly six months' trial, I have no hesitation in stating it to be decidedly the best among the many I have seen. Mounted on your Cylinder, it leaves nothing to be desired, WE BEING ENABLED BY IT TO CHARGE OUT EVEN FASTER THAN A CLERK CAN FIGURE.

Yours truly, W. KIRTLEY

(The Midland Company have since had a large number.)

JOHN BELLOWS, GLOUCESTER

John Buckingham and William Judd, were employed by him when he first set up on his own, and they were still working for the firm at the time of his death.

To facilitate easy calculation of the workers' wages, he invented a cylindrical calculator, a complicated apparatus which still survives, and which was evidently produced and marketed commercially. He also produced a pocket calculator which converted the metric system into English equivalents and vice versa. This device comprised four concentric circles of cardboard, and was envisaged as being useful to chemists and medical students. On the cover, he notes that the calculator "requires no writing except the answer". It was probably produced in 1870, for there is a letter from the Bishop of Gloucester (Nov. 14, 1870) noting that "The invention is most ingenious. I have a scientific friend coming to stay to whom I shall instantly show it and who, I am convinced, will be very pleased with it."

Having easy access to printing presses enabled John to publish his views on many different subjects as pamphlets. The first of these published in 1864, *Remarks on certain Anonymous Articles designed to render Queen Victoria unpopular*, was inspired by his sense of injustice to the Queen, following the appearance of scurrilous Palace gossip in a regular newspaper column. He felt that the Queen, whom he admired, was unable to answer the innuendos, which were made anonymously, so he took it upon himself to identify the writer. His evidence was flimsy and circumstantial: John Bright, the Quaker politician, whom he named, was known to have close connections with the *Morning Star*, the paper in which the column appeared, and the style of writing and public speaking were similar to that of the columnist. John published his 94-page account anonymously, after sending John Bright his name and address and asking for comments. John Bright failed to answer. A second edition of the pamphlet was brought out, this time, signed by the author. Towards the end of his life, John felt sorry for his impulsive action, but whether he was right or not, can never be known.

His interests were wide-ranging: there were religious tracts, *Ritualism or Quakerism*, *Who sent thee to baptize?*, *Why I ought not to keep 'Christmas'*, *Prayer*; offprints of the papers written for the Cotteswold Naturalists' Field Club and the Bristol & Gloucester Archaeological Society, and, later, of the American Antiquarian

Society. A Short account of *Two Days' excursion to Llanthony Abbey and the Black Mountains* in 1868 was followed by *A Week's holiday in the Forest of Dean* written with Colonel Holland in 1881. This successful guide was revised several times and the sixth edition was still in print in the 1950's.

There are few letters surviving from the 1870's: much time must have been taken up with the production of the first and second editions of the dictionary, but it is probable that he devoted more time to his family. By 1877 there were five children, Hannah and Philip being the two youngest. It is clear, from later letters, that the household was a lively one, with John much involved in his children's interests.

In 1879, Elizabeth wrote that John's health "had become somewhat impaired" and he was, with difficulty, persuaded to leave his home and business to go for a short trip to the Ardèche with his friend, William Lucy. Both were members of the Cotteswold Naturalists' Field Club and shared similar interests in Archaeology.

They first went to Vals, where he wrote to Elizabeth,

"I was so delighted with the walk we had after tea, on the way to Antraigues, that I could not help scheming all sorts of things to get thee over here with some of the children. I told William Lucy that I should not wish to see anything else but these valleys at Vals. Cliffs and hills, woodland and cascade succeeded each other at every bend of the road; while every now and then we came in view of the far shining snow-clad mountains high against the blue sky. They are intolerably beautiful.

I gathered bits of wild box to put in my letter home: bits of genista, violets, and I don't know what besides."

The next day he wrote again,

"We have just returned from a long drive to Montpesat, a large village some thirteen miles from Vals. Every part of the road is beautiful: all of it along valleys by the side of rivers, and all hemmed in by high granite hills whose lower slopes are cultivated in terraces, while the heights are clothed with chestnut trees.

The approach to Montpesat itself is grand. In front of us is a line of snowy mountains; at the left a mighty volcano, the cone of which is itself a mountain of red ash and cinder as high as Haresfield Hill above the railway, with trees on its lower part, and a few streaks of snow just at the summit; on our right, on the opposite side of the valley, a mighty hill forming a vast combe, in whose lower hollow nestled the town. To get to this we have to cross a suspension bridge over a chasm nearly as deep as Symonds Yat cliff.

It is now that I regret never having learned a little drawing; at any rate enough to make a difference between a forest tree and a besom! But a rough idea is better than an absolute blank."

The two men returned via Nimes to look at the Roman remains and amphitheatre, and then to Clermont Ferrand. From there he wrote,

"I am like a boy going home from school: ready to count the hours for my return. We have been up the Puy de Dôme, on the lower slopes of which grow pansies in abundance..... Very near the top we came upon the platform of a large temple erected by the Romans to Mercury, only lately discovered in building the observatory. It is all of chiselled lava - beautiful blocks of stone, many of which are as long as our front hall, and many of the steps cut deep out of a single stone. On all hands, and for hundreds of yards round, the soil is full of Roman pottery. I could have quickly filled a wheelbarrow with it."

John Bellows' drawing of Montpesat

38

CHAPTER VI

Quakers, Ireland and Family Life

IN WRITING TO JAMES GREEN of Worcester, another American friend, in 1882, John says,

"We have had a good deal of illness in our family ever since midsummer; five children, first and last, down with scarlet fever; which has delayed my acknowledging thy very acceptable letter .... but my wife in nursing three of them before we had the aid of a trained nurse, so utterly exhausted her strength that she has had a narrow escape of her life. I am glad to say she is now fairly well on the way to health again however; and while our house is, I believe, as healthy as a dwelling in the town can be - for the town is low and rather damp - I hope before long we may be able to live in the country, where a more bracing air will give us all more vigor."

During the next year they moved to Saintbridge House, halfway between Gloucester and Upton St. Leonards, whilst a new house was being built on Upton Hill, to be known as Upton Knoll. He describes this house in a further letter to James Green, mentioning that "When I broke down so utterly last Spring, as to be for some time incapable of any work, my wife wisely foresaw that the change to life in the country, and the change of occupation and interests involved in building a house, would be better for me..." The subsequent move was surely better, too, for Elizabeth and the family, and Upton Knoll remained their home until after his death. Built on the side of the hill, the house had splendid views across Gloucester to the Welsh mountains, the Wye and the Severn Bridge.

Upton Knoll House – sketch by George Charity

Severn Railway Bridge (later destroyed by fire)

It would seem that his breakdown was, perhaps, the most severe of the several bouts of depression from which he suffered in later life. It may partly explain why he left the Society of Friends at this particular time. This step, which must have been shattering to him and to Elizabeth and the family, is barely mentioned by her, but is described more fully in the *Gloucester Journal*'s obituary notice.

"He dissociated himself from the Society on account of certain modifications in the form of worship."

A contributory factor to his decision may well have been his quietest and mystical tendencies, which were in sharp contrast to the progressive and radical ideas prevalent at that time among Friends: the obituary writer notes that despite his differing opinions and convictions "no breach of friendship was possible to Mr. Bellows." He continued to associate with members of the Society, and he was granted the use of one of the rooms at Greyfriars where, with his family and a few friends, he continued to worship on Sunday afternoon, and, each mid-week, a similar meeting was held in his business premises. This splinter group was no doubt a headache to Gloucester Friends Meeting, but they seemed to have accepted it with generosity and understanding: we are not told of the strains and stresses which may well have existed.

As to his breakdown, in a later letter from Oliver Wendell Holmes (Jan. 28, 1885), a note of envy creeps in,

"I have to write so much that I get very tired, and I could not help thinking, as I read of your *breaking down*, how I should like to break down - for a little while..... A few weeks of absolute idleness would be a great blessing to me, but I am caught in the wheels of a promise, and round I must go".

After the family had moved to Upton Knoll, John worked in Gloucester only in the mornings and thus was able to spend the rest of the days at home, mostly in the garden, where he planned the lay-out of trees, shrubs, paths and beds - a practical and enjoyable occupation.

Unfortunately, this routine did not last long. In 1886, the Home Rule Bill for Ireland, was introduced to Parliament, which rekindled his fears of Catholicism. Sensing that its dominance in Ireland might threaten the religious freedom of other sects, he worried especially for his Protestant Irish friends. His prejudice was so great that it is instanced by ..... the obituary writer, who mentioned the case in which, as a printer ..... "he was asked to print some verses addressed to the Virgin Mary, in which she was described as the means through which the Soul is brought to Christ. A polite refusal led to a correspondence in which Mr. Bellows set out his views with great force. "No, I dare no more print these false suggestions, even for private reading, than I dare sell arsenic, on the assurance that it is only for the use of an habitué."

He was profoundly convinced that Home Rule would be disastrous for Ireland so he joined the local Liberal Unionist Association, and became its Treasurer. He, himself, contributed much of the Association's literature from his own pen, and was in wide correspondence with friends and fellow workers. To the archaeologist, Dr. Hübner of Berlin with whom he had been corresponding since he had discovered the Roman wall etc in Eastgate, "I may mention that in spite of my not being well-able to work more than a few hours daily, which are taken up with my printing business, I have taken an active part for the last twelve months in the exposure and combating of some of the fallacies of the Separatists who seek to sever Ireland from Britain. This, partly from the accident of my being a printer, and having the means at hand of circulating leaflets or bills on the subect, on a very large scale. Thus, during some eleven months I have printed and sent out some five millions of copies of such leaflets; and as some of these have been translations into Welsh and Gaelic (for the Highlands of Scotland) an idea has struck me that I may take advantage of the information obtainable through our distributors, to do what I believe has never yet been attempted - i.e. draw up a linguistic map of Great Britain." (This idea was never carried out.) When this political struggle was over, Lord Salisbury wrote (1895),

"I have heard so much of the great service you have rendered to the Unionist cause, not only recently, but for many years past, that I cannot refrain from writing to thank you warmly for them, on behalf of the Party, though I have not had the pleasure of your acquaintance...."

By the mid 1880's, the Bellows family had grown to eight: three more children had been born, Kitty (1880), Lucy (1881), and Jack (1883). A letter to Oliver Wendell Holmes (1885) gives a glimpse of their family life.

"Here at last is the moment of leisure for which I have long waited, that I might acknowledge thy kind gift of the *Memorials of Emerson*...... I have reserved the volume for reading aloud to my wife, which is a very slow process, because our available time is restricted to the intervals after tea. Even this has to be divided into sections to suit different auditories, whose tastes require different books..... After Lucy had gone to bed, things go pretty smoothly till half-past eight, when the rest follow, except our eldest boy. "Max hand me the Emerson: there it is, on the second shelf."

....."Oh do let me read this bit first, out of *Stories from Virgil!* I've been waiting all the evening to do it, and I have to return the book this week."

"*Nine o'clock*" Time for Max to stop; but he begs to finish the chapter ('only a few more pages,') and as he is in the middle of a terrible boxing-match, we let him go on till twenty-seven minutes past: by which time 'Dares' is dragged off the ground with his toes trailing after him, 'vomiting blood, and teeth in the blood.' It takes some minutes after the story is over to realise the inconsistency of such reading in the family circle, or semi-circle even; for had the same matter occurred in the newspaper, we should have turned away from it promptly.... And with this we come to Emerson.... it has interested us greatly."

He continues with an appreciation of Emerson and ends with "There's not enough for this and that". One assumes he meant Time.

In 1883, after the tiring months when he had been in the thick of the anti-Home Rule campaign, John was able to take both Elizabeth and Max, now 18 years old, on holiday abroad to Trèves to see the Roman remains there; to visit a friend in France whom he had met at Metz, and another friend in Germany. They also visited museums in Cologne, Bonn and Mannheim. We do not know how much these interested John's companions, but it is clear, from a letter to Oliver Wendell Holmes that Elizabeth enjoyed, especially, the warm hospitality of the French family and their thirteen-year old daughter.

The next autumn, they were off again, this time to visit Max who was now studying German in Leipzig, from where he wrote to his friend, Francis Michell (a friend from his Cornish childhood).

"Here I am on the Continent again, and, reminded by the circumstancs of the journey we once took together in Belgium ... it would be impossible, within the limits of even a long letter, to describe the places we have seen, but we have touched upon or run through parts of the Thuringian and Hartz forests as well as the Niederwald, covering some of the most beautiful scenery in the German Empire. The cream of the cream, barring the Rhine, is the country round Eisenach, in Thuringia - a district so closely associated with the history of Martin Luther, and therefore of modern Europe.... The real place for meeting with people of many different nationalities is the fair at Leipzig. For ages regarded as the great central point for Europe and Asia, the wares bought and

Bellows family picnic in about 1887
Back row (left to right): __?__, JOHN, __?__, Hannah
Front row: Kitty, Jack, Willie, Marian, Dorothy, ELIZABETH, Lucy

sold in it represented the industries of all lands, both East and West. Now most of the important business is no longer conducted in booths, but in buildings, such as the Booksellers' Exchange. This is a sort of clearing-house for all the booksellers in Germany, who come once a year to show all their new things, and to square up accounts for the year past."

Refreshed after their holiday on the Continent, John and his family - now increased to nine by the arrival of Dorothy (1885) - resumed their normal lives, and in a splendidly frank and affectionate exchange of letters with Oliver Wendell Holmes, we get a vivid picture of some aspects of this life.

John writes from Upton Knoll in 1891,

"Nothing is harder to realize than the flight of time. It seems but as the vivid yesterday that I was passing through the streets of London in a cab with thy daughter, who was on her way to take thee from one friend's house to that of another, in the crowd of engagements that filled up thy brief visit to England. Suddenly we turned out of the throng and bustle and in a few moments drew up before the mansion of James Russell Lowell, from whose company I had to send up a message to summon thee. As I stood in the hall I heard his voice, in a cheery leave-taking on the stair: the only time I ever heard it, though I had had some kindly written words from him anent my dictionary. The next moment I was shaking hands with thyself and receiving the greeting that was thereafter renewed in Gloucestershire..... There is one *adoucissement* that tells on us with increasing force as life advances - the society of little children..... I come home jaded and careworn from my work, and tempted to think my lot heavier than other men's: when my boy Jack comes marching up to me with a sort of box in his hand - four bits of board nailed together with brads and tin-tacks, and two thick wooden discs that he had routed out of some cupboard, to make a baker's cart. I wanted to sit and "rest" - that is, to brood over the miseries of my lot, but Jack cannot stay for brooding or anything else. He has been "waiting such a long time" for my coming home, to tell him how to saw these two wheels edgeways so as to make them into four; and how to put axles to them; and the end of it is that I have to set to work in good earnest, and, after long application of blunt tools and tool substitutes - the baker's cart is finished.

By this time I have begun to take a real interest in it. Next morning I buy a wooden horse that fits it; and another spell of work ensues in the fitting of his harness. Dorothy (five) has been busy in the kitchen making loaves to go in it for the load; and he and she and I drag it for miles along the sideboard and the dining table and the hall floor. In the course of the evening Jack asks me whether a mouse could pull the baker's cart. I tell him I think it could. Later on he wants to know how many flies are as strong as one mouse. Not foreseeing the bearing of the question, I reply somewhat carelessly, "Perhaps a hundred". Next morning I meet him marching about with a pasteboard box in his hand. "How do people feed flies?" "With sugar." "How much sugar would a hundred flies eat?" Now in strict truth I could not tell; but an answer must be given at once, and so I say "Oh, I should think a lump would last them three days." In a few minutes he is at my side again with the box. The lid is cautiously raised, and I am desired to look in. "I'm going to catch a hundred flies and tame them like the man did with the fleas, and make them draw the baker's cart. I've caught one. There he is!" I looked in. There was a large lump of sugar in the centre, and the fly pacing up and down past it with a nonchalant air as if it did not concern him what was done ....

The time at breakfast passed quickly, for I was plied with a variety of questions about the team of fleas I had at some time mentioned, that were trained by a man at Plymouth to draw a little coach, and with one of their own species sitting on the box as driver.

I must say I began to get uneasy, for I knew not whereunto this would grow, and I slipped off to the office with some new anxieties in my mind. At dinner the crisis came. "Papa, how do they *tame* flies?" I was in a dilemma; and at last, I was forced to confess that I did not know. "And, besides," I hurried on to add, "I don't know how we can harness them. I could not tie knots small enough to hold them without hurting them." There was a pause of disappointment. Jack's whole scheme was breaking down. He had looked upon me as able to do anything, if I only tried; and now I had failed him. Revolving the whole altered position in his mind, he at last said: "What had I better do with the fly that is in the box? Perhaps I had better let him go?" I caught at the idea and assented. The fly himself had come to the same conclusion a little earlier, for when Jack lifted the lid he had already gone! I heaved a sigh of relief. But it was premature. "Wouldn't a mouse be easier to harness than a hundred *flies*?" "Well, yes, I think it would." "Then I'll go and ask William to set the trap in the stable and catch me one." ..... Many days passed..... Suddenly, one afternoon, we were startled by a shout from a number of voice in different high keys, "*Jack's mouse is caught!*" All the rest of the day "my mouse" was the object of lavish attentions; and I last saw him before he retired for the night; he had stacked by his side, as much cheese and tallow-candle ends as it would take him four days to eat. "Does he like being in the box?".... "Well - no. He would rather be able to run about." In the morning he brought me the box, stored as it had been overnight with cheese and ends of candle, but no occupant was in it. "Why, Jack! where's the mouse?" "Oh, I thought it would be ra'r cruel to keep him in; so I took him to the stable and let him go."

From another letter to O.W.H. dated 1890,

"Dear Friend, Which chord shall I touch to begin with, as I rise from the first few delightful hours reading of thy book?.... One mystery thy volume has set me further away than ever from solving, and that is, where is the boundary between childhood and boyhood, or boyhood and manhood and age? This I have never been able to find.... Only this very evening I was wheedled into an interlude from the "Teacups" by a deputation of four Gallios who care for none of these things, to entreaties that I would "give them a chase". Seven-year-old put the request in a very low voice, for a chase, in this house, is forbidden by the Mistress on the grounds that it makes a Dust; it destroys the Carpets; it leaves Finger-Marks on the Walls; it Tears the Clothes; it upsets the Furniture with other high crimes and misdemeanours which are duly set forth in the manifesto which forbids chasing indoors. So, like Shelley's "sweet child sleep", seven-year-old "murmers like a noontide bee"; while ten-year-old and five-year-old and eight-year-old keep furtively glancing at the Arbitress of their fate to make sure that she does not overhear what is going on. And so

> A spirit in my feet
>
> Has led me, who knows how,

out of the room - these four stealing silently after me till we get to the foot of the stairs, when off they go like hares, I following - into the bathroom, and the day nursery, and the night nursery, and down the back stairs, for dear life! Everyone I can catch is swept off to prison, either tucked under my arm, or dragged by the heels along the floor, according to weight and size. (It doesn't hurt the carpets a bit! It's only a superstition of the mistress. They look fresher than ever after it.) And all this time there is a din of voices in calls and shouts and shrieks, *à tue-tête* as the French say! By and by a message comes from the Mistress that the chase has lasted long enough; that we must all come into the dining-room, that it is Dorothy's bedtime..... Why, here is a game older than Adam! The old hunting instinct of the cave-man coming down to us by heredity, an instinct that has scores of times transformed me into a cave-bear under the dining-room table.... I do not think that anything in this life has more puzzled me than this consciousness that the bond between boyhood and manhood

      Is marked by no distinguishable line

      The turf unites; the pathways intertwine.

Now and then in my morning walk to Gloucester I have enjoyed the company of Freddie Matthews, aged eight, on his way to school. No ceremony is needed to step into conversation with him, any more than to step into a horse-car while it is going; and the like freedom prevails in leaving the one as the other.

"We killed our pig last week."

"Was he fat?"

"Ay, ten score. Father weighed 'un back in June and he was eight score, and then he weighed 'un again in a bit-a-while and he was more'n nine score. So, soon as he was ten score, Father killed 'un."

"Indeed! And what has he done with him?"

"Salted 'un in. He've put the sides in Grandfather Ponting's."

"What's that for?"

"Cause hee's house is drier'n ours."

Before I could assert this information and store it away for reference in my mind under the article "Pig", Freddie suddenly whipped out of his pocket a top and held it up triumphantly under my eye.

"What's that?"

"A top. Our Harry made 'un out of a bobbin for Syd."

48

"And how old is Syd?"

"Three year old. He made the peg with a nail he found."

"Will it spin?"

(Scornfully) "Ay! a lot better than them there boughten ones."

"But why is he better than a boughten one?"

"Cause when they goes down they lies there, but after he's down HE'LL JUMP UP AGAIN IF YOU GIVES 'UN A GOOD HARD HIT and go on just the same as he was afore!.... LOOK-EE HERE!" and he hopped off the path into the middle of the road, and gave the transformed bobbin a tremendous smack. It gave a feeble stagger and fell. One more rousing smack - I looking on in breathless excitement to see it jump up again - but it lay still as if stunned by the blow.

In a bated tone Freddie said "He didn't do it THAT TIME, but HE WILL!" and slipped it into his pocket as he sprang back to my side on the footpath.

A fortnight after this I was again walking to Gloucester. I met Grandfather Ponting, as I often do, at the bottom of Mason Pitch (all gentle slopes in Gloucestershire are "pitches"), carrying two buckets of mash for the nephews of the pig who was salted in. In the garden gateway of Matthews' cottage stood a little boy with a perfectly circular face, large-eyed, and very red in the cheeks, a sort of cheruborustic. I found this was Syd. Freddie's face is oval, not quite so ruddy or so perfectly free from all trace of care.

In a few moments I overtook the latter, and the instant I was abreast of him I broached the subject that had often been in my thoughts since our last walk.

"How's the top going on that Harry made out of a bobbin?"

"Oh! he's lost. Syd's got a new 'un."

"LOST?"

"Ay! he lost'un .... and then he found 'un .... and then he lost 'un again."

Before I could recover from the strain put on me by the vivid realization of the alternations of trouble and hope and disappointment involved in this series of changes, Freddie drew from his pocket a bright magenta-tinted top with a glittering tin-tack at its point. I

49

saw at a glance that this was no home made article. There was a professional touch about it that told of the toy factories of the Black Forest.

"What did it cost?"

"A farthin'. Syd found a farthin' by the pigsty and our Harry went into Gloucester to spend 'un for 'im, and bought HE" (Four miles - two each way, for Harry.) I remembered the comparison that had been made between the now lost top and "boughten ones" to the disadvantage of the latter, and I felt some misgiving as I asked;

"Will he spin as well as the one Harry made with the bobbin and nail?"

"Ay, A LOT BETTER'N HE."

Optimism? It is not a strong word to describe the continual flow of cheeriness which carries this boy of eight through the ups and downs of his career. It was with a smile he told me of his week's stay at home from school "because Mother's bad, got the Brown Kitis, and her head's bad." With a smile he related how "Father chopped open his hand with the bill-hook, and had to go into the Infirmary to have it sewed up, and to-day he's gone in again to have the tackin' took out."

Two or three years have slipped away since this, and I see Grandfather Ponting's hair getting whiter; as my own is becoming what his used to be. Syd's face is distinctly no longer quite round, but I one day caught sight, inside the gate, of one just like it only smaller, and more than a circle in its outline. Freddie, standing near, had a bandage over one eye.

"What's the matter?"

He looked up, quite pleased, with the other, and replied, "A ball hit 'un." When some weeks had gone by and the bandage was still in its place, I felt a hearty sorrow for the boy; but he showed no sign of sharing it, for as I was driving past I slackened the reins to ask, "How is thy eye, Fred?" "Any better?"

"No, nor never won't be, no more!" and turned away in undisguised pleasure*.

* Both these extracts were taken from letters selected by Lord Birkenhead for his *The 500 Best English Letters* published in 1931.

The sad, last letter from Oliver Wendell Holmes, from Boston 1891, begins "My dear Mr. Bellows, You must not think that I have forgotten you, or lost my interest in your delightful letters, because you have not heard from me for a good while. The truth is writing is becoming more and more troublesome to me on account of the state of my eyes..... But oh, how lonely the world is getting to look! While Lowell* was living I felt his friendship was a strong tie to my past: now that has snapped, and Whittier and I are, as I said to him the other day, on a spar together, floating still, remnants of a raft which has gone to pieces..... Write to me whenever you feel like it without waiting for *answers*, which must grow few and shorter as the tide of old age flows about the chair of the octogenarian as the ocean around that of King Canute.

Always faithfully and cordially yours

O.W. Holmes

"I always find your details of home-life, especially of the younger people of your acquaintance, the best of reading." O.W.H. died three years later, in 1894.

Courtesy
George Routledge
London 1888

* James Russell Lowell, the founder (in 1857) and editor of the *Atlantic Monthly*. (First mentioned p. 45.)

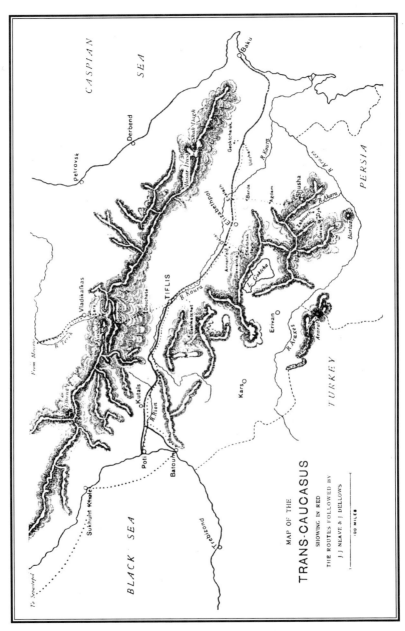

Map of Caucasus

MAP OF THE

TRANS-CAUCASUS

SHOWING IN RED

THE ROUTES FOLLOWED BY

J J NEAVE & J BELLOWS

100 MILES

CASPIAN SEA

BLACK SEA

PERSIA

TURKEY

TIFLIS

Baku

Derbend

Petrovsk

Vladikakas

Kutais

Poti

Batoum

Sukhum Khale

To Sevastopol

Trebizond

Kars

Erivan

Ararat

R. Araxes

R. Rion

R. Koura

R. Koura

Elizabethpol

Geoktchaik

Shusha

R. Akara

Bardanujoky

Shah-Yaigh

Dushete

Baina

Batumnet

L. Goktcha

Ardebil

CHAPTER VII

Russia, The Caucasian Exiles

THE SOCIETY OF FRIENDS has, since its beginning, held that no religious work or service should be undertaken unless it be inspired by an inward, spiritual prompting. A 'concern', a specific mission would be brought before fellow Members so that the matter could be fully considered, and either accepted or discouraged by them.

In 1891, Joseph Neave, an English Friend living in Australia, felt just such a 'concern' for a Russian Protestant sect, the Stundists, who were being persecuted and driven from their homes. Their pacifist beliefs ran counter to those of the Greek Orthodox Church and to the Government, since they refused military service.

At first Joseph was asked by his meeting to wait a year, but, in 1892, he personally brought the matter to London, to the Quaker Yearly Meeting, and his concern was accepted. Usually, such a mission was carried out with a companion, but Joseph was prepared to go alone as his plans were so uncertain. John Bellows heard of this mission and felt called to accompany Joseph. Although John was worried about leaving Elizabeth and his family for an indefinite time, she encouraged him to offer his companionship to Joseph. Divine prompting and, no doubt his love of adventure, helped him in his decision.

Despite the fact that he was no longer officially in Membership of the Society, the Arrangement Committee considered that his past record of service and travel made him ideal for this delicate and vague mission, even though he was now 61 years old.

John and Joseph needed further knowledge of the location of the exiles (Stundists, and other pacifist sects, including Doukhabors, Molokans and Mennonites). Once in Russia, they were frequently delayed by difficulties in contacting the authorities who could enlighten them and, in addition, those who could give them the necessary permission and assistance with their travels.

John's letters home give graphic descriptions of their journeys, but, understandably, personal letters lack details of interviews with officials and visits to the dissenters. Joseph, writing his account fifteen years later, provided much missing information.

On October 12, 1892, the two men left England for St. Petersburg, travelling by rail via Cologne and Koenigsberg. When they arrived, they obtained an interview with Pobedonstov, the Procurator of the Greek Church Synod, said to be the most powerful man in Russia. Because of his merciless persecution of all dissenters he was known as the Torquemada of the Nineteenth Century. However, he received them "very pleasantly" and the two Friends "spoke freely with him on the subject we had at hand; namely, the right of every human being to worship and serve God in whichever way he considered best." The Procurator was surprisingly sympathetic to them, doubtless because he had met several English Quakers during the previous year, when Friends had provided substantial relief to the Volga area for the famine which had followed a series of poor harvests.

John and Joseph also made contact with Ministers of State, and were invited to the British Embassy: they had intended to request an introduction to the Ambassador whilst in England, but deemed it best to "trust to the Lord". In fact, a chance meeting with the Ambassador's daughter, at the home of a Russian friend, resulted in a very friendly interview with the Ambassador who showed sympathy to their cause. "He reminded me of an old lion, quiet and majestic" wrote John.

Once they had the blessing of the authorities, they were able to leave St. Petersburg. An article in the newspaper *Novosti*, attacked them as "two Quakers from England who have come to Russia to force an open door - inasmuch as there is already full liberty of conscience in Russia"!

Caucasus Travelling Trio
left to right: Herman Fast (interpreter), Joseph Neave and John Bellows

Leaving St. Petersburg, they travelled by rail to Moscow, taking their interpreter Herman Fast with them. Whilst in Moscow, they visited Count Tolstoy, who had become spokesman for the dissenters, no doubt protected from police harassment by his social position. He and his family welcomed them warmly, and, for John, this was the beginning of a growing friendship, which lasted until John's death, despite fundamental differences in their points of view.

They left Moscow and, at last, were on their way to the Caucasus, travelling by train to Vladikafkas. "To travel on continuously from night till morning, and again till morning wears into evening ..... gives one to realise the immensity of the Russian Empire...... it was really enjoyable to stand on the platform at the end of the carriage. The morning air was sweet, and the train was speeding away over the steppe; back as far as the limit of the horizon, and on as far as the eye could reach, one vast wilderness of dark brown, not exactly like a moorland, for there is hardly vegetation enough for that, yet like a moorland that has no beginning or end..... when we reached Vladikafkas, 2300 feet above the sea, the air had a mountain feel about it that was not unpleasant. The people now began to look far more foreign, dark Armenian and Tartar countenances, strange great white wool caps, long bourkas or cloaks of coarse black goats' hair: women with shawls over their heads - children padded to a rotundity that would amaze some of you at home."

In this town, then the capital of Northern Caucasus, the two Friends found many Stundist exiles, all under police surveillance: their churches had recently been closed and they were far away from their own homes. In a private house at nightfall, a small group gathered secretly to meet the two Quakers. "As these few came in - middle-aged men - they shake hands and kiss us, Russian fashion..... One of the Russians prays in a very humble and broken spirit, and is followed by another in the same true power and feeling. I do not remember ever to have been in such an assembly...... After the meeting was over, tea was placed on the table with a beautiful pile of rusks and glasses of preserved cherries which they put into the tea, and very nice they are."

After a few days, they went on by 'omnibus'. "The total length of the road (from Vladikafkas) to Tiflis is 200 versts, or 133 English miles.... We are to start at 3 o'clock the following afternoon, and to travel all night with four horses, changing them at twelve stations, with additional ones at three or four of the hardest gradients. The omnibus was to take one inside passenger besides ourselves, and one outside. The inside passenger presently made his appearance - a powerfully-built Georgian of over six feet in height, with features exactly like those carved on the Assyrian monuments.... the outside passenger was a little man; a Jew, of over eighty years of age, who took his place between the driver and the conductor. All our luggage being loaded left barely room for the four of us to squeeze in with it." Later, the luggage was moved outside, and the old man, who had become icy cold and near to death, was accommodated inside.

At one turn where a mountain higher than Ben Nevis suddenly loomed above us, I made some exclamation... the Georgian gave a glance at the snowy peak, and said depreciatingly, 'That's nothing! It's a *malo* - a *malinky*! (a little one - a little mite of a thing). Wait till you get further on, to the *bolshoi* (big) cliffs. Then you will see things that will nearly break your neck to bend back and look up at!'

After a while the distant lights of a great city become visible among the environing mountains ..... we drop to a slow walk as our horses climb a steep hill - then gallop down: up again: and we are in a wide street of the city."

Now in Tiflis, they were again delayed because the Governor of the area, was away, so they had no choice but to await his return. This gave them the opportunity to explore the city in a leisurely way. By chance, two days after their arrival, they met the old Jew again: he was delighted to see them, saying that he and his wife wished 'you might live to *five times your present age*'. The old couple were most solicitous, giving them hospitality and introducing them to the rest of their family and to members of the Jewish community.

John and Joseph had time to wander about, and John was fascinated by the sights and sounds around him. He describes a typical Tiflis scene thus, "We cross the narrow street, hopping from one high cobble to another. A horse passes, with two disgusting-looking greeny wet skins distended: each skin squirting a fine spray of water about a yard long, at anyone who has a mind to get in the way......

'Ding, ding, ding,' I heard at a little distance, but paid no attention to it - for seven donkeys had come round the corner laden with charcoal, and so laden that each donkey formed a sort of imitation camel. As these animals have no idea of method, they spread all across the street in loose marching order, one of them putting me to the instant alternative of letting him charcoal my coat on the left, or else of my rubbing it on the right against the bloody neck of a sheep whose carcase swung pendulum-wise from a butcher's shop. By a sharp skip I avoided both Scylla and Charybdis, and then stepped into a shop space to let a blind man pass, who being stout of person took up the available foot-path - vaguely extending his hands on each side in advance of him, and holding his forehead back to catch, it might be, some gleam of the blessed light of which in this bazaar there was none too much for those who *had* eyes. A rogue of a boy (all boys are rogues) gave him a bump for the pleasure of seeing him waggle - which he did, and then recovered his balance ..... an angry shouting and clang of bell came from behind. I turned, and there was a tram-car swinging round the corner, loaded with Armenians, Turks, ladies, officers, and I know not what besides, all nearly brought to a dead stand...... The fact was that the mud had so hidden the tram-line that I had no idea there was one there at all!"

The two Friends discovered that the local gaol was open to the public and they made use of this at least twice to visit prisoners: they were thus able to talk to exiles, waiting to be moved to their permanent quarters in villages up in the mountains.

They also saw prisoners in the street. John writes, "In the market place we met an étape - that is a gang of perhaps twenty manacled prisoners, under a guard of twelve soldiers. The street was steep; and it was a new and painful sight to see this throng of grey-clad men, and to hear the heavy clank of their irons as they marched past."

When the Governor returned and they were, eventually, granted an interview, he was sympathetic and permitted them to go where they pleased, only stipulating that they should not hold meetings nor distribute literature; they were usually to be accompanied by a Government official. Moreover, he advised them to wait yet another week for the District Governors' Annual Meeting, and to make a point of seeing the Governor of Elisabethpol province, where most of the Stundists lived. They were given much practical assistance in arranging their future journeys, which were to take them, on fearful roads, into distant areas high in the Caucasus.

At the end of January 1893, they left Tiflis, when John wrote: "It is with a feeling of relief that I find myself again on the railway, as it means one more step towards the accomplishment of our work." They were now on their way to Daliar, where they hoped to pick up transport to the copper mines at Kedabek and thence to some villages high up in the Caucasus.

On their arrival, he wrote, "We found our bedroom at Daliar last night cold enough to make our *bourkas* valued as a covering.... The whole premises is so arranged as to serve as the store for the copper, etc., and the upper part as a kind of hotel for persons coming to and from the mines. The agent is a German of perhaps thirty five years of age - a bright active man, with a bright wife, and one little girl three years old. They were abounding in their efforts to make us comfortable. As to Clara, two things heightened us much in her opinion. The first was a box of a Russian sweetmeat, made from apple-jelly into a sort of Turkish delight.... The second was a happy acquirement of Joseph Neave's, by which a handkerchief, knotted, is drawn over the top of the forefinger to make a man, the knot forming his cap. In so lonely a position as this home in the steppe, where a child of three has no playmate of her own age, thou wilt fancy how popular all this would make us!

We are to be called at 6.30, and start as soon as we have had coffee. The distance is 45 versts - 30 miles - over the mountains; and with six horses (and even they are useless over the steepest three versts, which we walk) it will take us till six o'clock at night to reach Kedabek.... By degrees the way rose as it wound to and fro over the moorland, in front was a line of mountains, serrated into hundreds of points, all glistening with snow - larger ones behind the smaller. As hour after hour passed, we rose higher and higher into scenery that now reminded one of Malvern, and now of the Welsh mountains. At last the slant is steeper than even six horses can manage ..... and we take off our wraps and walk for three versts. By midday the sharp pointed hills have given place to great rounded mountains..... Daylight had gone, and with it the only sign of life, except now and then a wagon or peasant on the road, a kind of crow, and the snow-bunting. The last time I saw this bird was on Ben Nevis. But I ought not to have missed mention of Tchardachle - the Tartar village. It consisted partly of huts built of stone, with earthen roofs, and partly of caves or houses made in the ground, exactly as Strabo* describes the Caucasians 1900 years ago. He also says the people here had dogs as large and fierce as lions; and it made me start as I looked across the way from one of these subterranean houses, to see two dogs guarding each his master's door, immense in size, the exact colour and appearance of lionesses."

Just before reaching Kedabek, they came to a Doukhabor village. These people had been taken from their homes, to the Crimea, then transported to their present location. They were luckier than many exiles in that they had been given some land, and were able to be reasonably self-sufficient. Many exiles depended solely on their friends and relatives for their survival. In Kedabek itself other exiles were being harassed by the 'Missioner', sent from St. Petersburg to convert them to the Orthodox religion.

Their enforced delay in Kedabek gave the Friends the opportunity to see the mines, and John writes, "The mines are high in the mountainside, and the ore is brought down to be smelted, etc. All the processes are now performed with raw or unrefined petroleum from Baku. The mine was discovered ages ago, beyond history..... As it was not possible to go further during the afternoon, the manager of the mines asked if we would not occupy the time by going underground.... ...It was very warm in some of the 'backs'; but the mine is really well ventilated. They use the same methods as in Cornwall: powder for blasting the softer rock, and dynamite for the harder. An hour and a quarter of the underground journey was as much as we cared for.

On Third-day morning we started for two villages still higher in the mountains than Kedabek..... At the door stood a wagon - springless - with four little horses harnessed abreast and a bronzed peasant for driver. By the good offices of men accustomed to load goods, I was heaved up and got seated on a bundle of hay, as were the rest - and off we went. In a very brief time we found our wagon

* The Greek geographer 63BC-24AD, who recorded his travels in many volumes.

more comfortable than the phaeton. As for springs, the hay and our *shubas* answered. Real steel springs could not have stood such work as we had to go through. After a long climb up hill, we descended a steep hill, past a commenced but unfinished bridge across a gorge. Recollect, everything is deep in snow, and the brooks part frozen and part free. People talk about keeping a good heart. I thought later on in the day 'The best place to keep it is in one's mouth, for it keeps on coming there'."

Arriving at the villages, they found some fifty exiles living there and they were relieved to see that the local Tartars, although extremely poor themselves, were friendly and had allowed the "Christian Brethren" the use of a small piece of land. The Friends were treated as guests, and were well-cared for, but they were saddened to learn that the dread 'Missioner', whose methods of persuasion were far from gentle, had threatened to visit the dissenters.

Having completed their work in the Kedabek district, the party returned to Daliar, and from here, John wrote, "Soon, as we rose on to the high ground, we got a peep at the Great Caucasus mountains sixty versts away ... the whole vast wall of towering Alps stood in dazzling splendour before us - two hundred miles long and eleven thousand feet high! Far too wide to be comprehended in one view, the eye had to travel slowly along the great arc..... We are ourselves standing on a mountain at this outer line two thousand feet higher than the plain below our feet - the plain that rolls away westward to Europe and eastward to Asia; itself a great and vast indescribable sea of violet that ends nowhere, right or left, but dies away into violet mist, and that again into blue haze - and the blue haze into a grey that is again immeasurable - and then above all this the innumerable peaks and towers and cliffs, dazzling white against the far pale blue sky. White with faint blushes of palest rose colour, marked with thousands and tens of thousands of folds and wrinkles and lines running down from the snow into the violet sea of nothingness in the plains below. Yonder, far, very *very* far on the western horizon is Kasbek, 16,000 feet high."

The little party travelled on by train from Daliar to Elisabethpol, where they were able to replenish their stocks. Thence they went further east, by rail, to Udzharri, where they were given hospitality by James Brown, a Gloucester man whom they had encountered

Mount Kasbek c.16,000 ft. altitude   *Dangerous mountain path negotiated on horseback: see p. 66*

by chance in Tiflis: he worked as an engineer in the large Liquorice Factory there. John's letter continues, "This is Second-day, the 6th of Second-month. I was not very well this morning, and Joseph Neave and Fast begged me to stay in and rest - which I have done - while they paid the visit to Geoktchaiskaya, 17 versts from here. They have returned, and we have all been taken over the Liquorice Factory - a very interesting sight.... From the balcony in front, a splendid view of the Karabagh mountains."

The travellers now came to the most dangerous and difficult part of their journey. Writing on February 7th, 1893, John says, "When I posted my No. 45 into the mail carriage at Udzharri at seven this morning, I not only foresaw that some days must elapse before I could again get a letter on to the line of rail for home, but I thought that I should be some time before I had anything fresh to tell. But I am writing this under the strangest circumstances of the whole journey: lodging the night in an oriental caravanserai" [an unfurnished inn, within a compound giving shelter to travellers and their animals].

"At Evelach we found our Government attendant waiting for us. He had been kind enough to hire for us, as requested, two phaetons (the carriage of the country, though not well suited to it) each with four little horses abreast. Dividing our baggage between them, Fast and the attendant took one, and we the other. The agent's name is Gregoriowitch; a very decent young fellow. He is armed to the teeth, carrying besides his bright weapons, a breech-loading rifle and twenty-two rounds of ammunition..... As a heavy robbery took place on the road we are now travelling, only two months ago, Gregoriowitch wanted us to take an armed Cossack guard, which we promptly declined to do.

The robbery was between this posting station and the next (Agdam) to which we meant to push on to-night; but our drivers are so frightened that we have given up the attempt. Eight armed Tartars managed the whole affair. They began in the morning by stopping a phaeton; lashing the passengers to trees (for we are in a sort of straggling wood) and robbing them.... Yesterday they again robbed the mail near this spot!

Don't be uneasy on our account. The very fact of this letter arriving will show that I have posted it! But more than all we are under a higher protection than police. Arriving at the caravanserai... we are asked to climb a step-ladder to the gallery, and are shown into the upper room on the right - our quarters for the night; as the apartment below is for our drivers. The room itself has an earthen floor, and bare stone walls and bare timber flat roof above. We unpack, and when the samovar comes we make a splendid tea, the foundation of which is four cakes of Tartar bread which we bought at three kopeks a pound. Then we have sardines, butter, cheese and other luxuries."

The next morning, "We have just breakfasted. The room is as warm as toast, and we shall go out in the frosty air with a stock of heat that will last us the rest of the journey - 54 versts to Shusha - a Persian fortress - now belonging to Russia. It is walled and the gates are shut at night."

On the next stage to Shusha, he writes, "A good many camels have met us; and wagons, loaded with carpets and other merchandise. I never imagined when we left England that part of our work would lie in Persia; but so it is - for all this district was a Persian Province until the time of the Emperor Nicholas, I think. Almost everything is oriental in the extreme. We met two or three women this morning, of the poorer class, yet each veiled in silk. One was carrying her baby on her back and leading a little fellow by the hand."

At one stage, "We walked three versts before our folk overtook us as we wound in and out among the deep centres and lateral valleys of this wonderful series of volcanoes. One crater on our left was almost perfect; and basalt and lava on all hands told their own tale.

We caught sight of Shusha again and again for two hours or more before we reached it. It is right on top of a mountain, a thousand feet higher than Snowdon, above the plain of the Koura.

At last we find our road (which is new) passes through a breach forty feet wide made for it through the city wall - and we drive up the frozen street; wind again to and fro amid the quaintest old buildings, many in ruins, through the bazaar, out-Tiflis-ing Tiflis itself - and after a mile of such entanglements, pull up in a square or market place. Several hundreds of men and boys all surround us and offer counsel and comment in Persian, in Russian, in Armenian, and in Tartar, till the whole sound is as of a swarm of bees. Presently an Armenian and several men and boys under his rule, take each an article of our baggage, and we follow in the tail of their procession up a side street for a few yards, through a door, up an open staircase to a balcony, whence we are conducted to a comfortable room.

The Samovar comes; and we order fried fish for supper, with a little *shisslik* - roast bits of mutton done on the coals. An hour and a half after we have drunk our tea, it comes! But it is good - and we are thankful for the journey has been extremely fatiguing.

Fifth-day morning ...... We have had an excellent night's rest, notwithstanding the difference between European, or rather English, and Asiatic beds. The latter, here, are hard benches with a couple of rugs laid on them, no mattress, and one sheet...... When we arrived last evening we wanted a wash. There is only one basin

64

and ewer for the establishment - kept in a room open to the balcony on one side, outside our door. Now this boy (their attendant) not only poured a few spoonfuls into the hands of each of us in turn; but after we had all washed and the water was black, he quietly put the jug to stand in it and left it for the night."

The two men spent a day in Shusha with a group of exiles, one of whom, described by Joseph as "a fine old man of 80 whose white hair lay on his shoulders, and his venerable beard came nearly to his waist, reminding me of my ideal of the Patriarch Abraham.

After a busy day yesterday, we rose at five this morning to get an early breakfast and start for Gerusi- a journey of eighty versts, which by using the post-horses, we hope to finish by night.... The streets of Shusha are as steep as the worst parts of Stroud or Redruth; and as we drove uphill our horses slipped and scrambled in all directions on the ice ... but we soon got on better. A long descent followed, over deeply trampled and rutted mud, frozen as hard as stone - and on which we danced up and down till I began to wonder what might be the limit of shaking that the human diaphragm can bear..... By one o'clock we had reached the second stage, Abdalyarsha, again on a parting ridge of very high ground.... We find all the post-horses are gone from the station. We have the right to the first that come in; but they must have two hours rest. Meantime a fire is lighted in the station room ... and the samovar brought. We make a good meal; and then Joseph Neave and I decide to walk on...... At last we come out into a valley of nearly a verst in width, and the loud sound of water warns us that we can go no further till the wagons come up with us. We are on the banks of the River Akara - a fast-rushing stream of some two feet in depth, and from 50 to 100 feet wide ... our road goes on in many a loop and double S until we are at a dizzy elevation, looking down on the river below ... and we are running on snow, with alternations of sheet ice.... Our driver is rather less careful than some we have had, and he swings along in a happy-go-lucky way that keeps me nervous for our wheels skid sideways on the smooth ice sometimes. But at last we are descending again - and we are in the Stantsie Zabouch. Here we must sleep; and here we learn for the first time that we can go no further on wheels. We have still some fifty versts to go, to reach Gerusi; and as the post road is blocked, we are told we must go on horseback.

We open our door wide to the morning sunshine, at six o'clock, and again I enjoy the loud sound of the stream. We must cross the little river, and there is no bridge, so we all mount horses and wend our way to the bank... One after another our horses crept down the steep bank to the river, and got across among the rolling boulders. Then in Indian file we entered a gorge in the mountain opposite .... we went on climbing the edges of such steeps, sometimes 200 or 300 feet above the valley below.... One slab of rock took up all the path but six inches. It was covered with marks of scratches from horseshoes; but a real slip would have sent horse and rider hopelessly into the ravine below. When we had got to about two thousand feet higher than the village, we were glad to get out of the precipice path on to a great table-land of snow of but gentle slope..... We came to a sort of dyke, down which my horse was picking his way carefully and safely, when the Tartar stole up behind and gave him a whack that made him start and miss a foothold. He did not actually fall, but plunged so that I should have gone over his head but for the pommel of the saddle - one of the best things among this barbarous people. It is a real handle, and an instant grip of this saved me."

Both John and Joseph dismounted for the long steep descent to the crowded Armenian village of Dyk. Mounted again, in the village, John wrote, "We could barely give room to the men who were standing in the 'street' - if I must call it a street - without endangering our horses foothold. Worst of all was a little donkey loaded with firewood.... If I rode outside of him he would push me over the cliff; if inside, I should send him over. I kept patiently behind him till he got to a little passing place.

After more ups and downs we again come out on a plateau covered with snow; and look down some couple of thousand feet below on Gerusi.... At last we got to the valley, and in a few minutes were in the yard of the caravanserai. As it is a fine sunny afternoon we unloaded our luggage in the yard and sat outside while a Tartar youth wiped our floor with a wet cloth, and cleaned the little table."

The Friends stayed the next day with the exiles, some thirty-five of them, ten with wives and children; without land they were totally dependent on the goodwill of others.

Before leaving Gerusi, they walked to the Armenian Village described by John, "It is a place of exceeding interest - there are

66

500 houses, part of them half underground in the slant of the hill, and part caves cut in the towers and spires of sandy conglomerate that cover the mountain side. I begged permission to go into one of these houses. A parley with two veiled women seemed likely to fail, when fortunately the husband came home in the nick of time .... it was intensely interesting to sit down on the carpeted bench in a cave-dwelling, and see the ancient loom and spinning wheel as old as the Babylonian Empire; and the oven in the middle of the floor; and many things besides."

Now the travellers started on their downward journey. John and Joseph preferred to walk back to Dyk trusting their own feet rather than their horses': in fact Joseph, later, chose to walk on from there to Zabouch, Herman Fast accompanying him on horseback whilst John and the Armenian took the troika.

Describing the journey from Shusha to Gerusi, John wrote, "No one can form the least idea of the difficulty of such a journey as this to Gerusi ... by looking at the map, which gives it forty versts as the crow flies; whereas the actual measured distance on the post road is eighty. And the to and fro of this eighty versts takes the same time that it does from *London to Petersburg* - four days! while it is incomparably more fatiguing than to travel from England to Russia!" The travellers spent little time in Shusha, but pushed on, visiting Agdam, a Tartar settlement, on the way. Here, John wrote, "I am as well as need be, yet aching in every limb from the tremendous jolting of the last few days... There is no fear of being robbed just here, for the police are at this moment scouring the district after the band whose exploits I have already told..... The stage was twenty versts. I had walked seven or eight when Joseph Neave overtook me, and at ten versts the carriages overtook us. The fact is that walking is far more pleasant than riding, for the bitter cold north wind was blowing in our faces from the Daghestan Mountains; and the exercise just balanced the chill.

It is a cold chilly evening as we drive past the caravanserais with their silhouetted mosquito towers to the Evelach Railway Station. We have to ask permission of the authorities to be allowed to stay in the waiting-room all night, for there is no train westward till half-past eight to-morrow morning. There is a train to Baku at ten at night; several passengers drop in, and we have a very interesting chat with one of them, a Tartar formerly in the body-guard of

Alexander II. He is a thin intelligent-looking man, shaved all but a heavy moustache, a strict Mahometan. I do not know that I ever gained more information from any man in the same brief interval than from him."

The travellers spent a comfortless night ... a fire had been lit but went out during the night. Despite this, John slept well in his wolf-skin coat; the others fared less well, all except the station cat which snuggled up beside James, warmed by his bourka. In the morning "a few passengers came in: among them a *Priestoff* or superintendant of police, in his grey uniform. As he opens the door, he falls all along, dead drunk on the floor."

In the train to Tiflis, John wrote a note to Elizabeth about his letters and also about his fits of despair, "I sat up very late last night writing the foregoing. On glancing at it I note that it conveys the exact impressions of the moment; yet it would mislead a stranger to our movements if he imagined they were mainly light or amusing. I purposely avoid much mention of such parts of our work as involve mental pain and exercise of spirit. These are neither few nor far between. Such a season was my lonely walk from Barda; heaved up and down on the wave, I could well feel near the state of the disciples who cried, 'Master, carest thou not that we perish?' Yet, above it all, and below it all, is the feeling that it will yet be well; and one is held firmly enough in the storms not to cast away the small measure of confidence that is left till the waves grow still again.

I did not mention yesterday the beautiful blue seas we saw under the Koura cliffs. They set me dreaming, as well they might, for they were of dream material themselves - a mirage - with the morning sun on the vapour."

Back in Tiflis, writing on 20th February, "Yesterday, First-day, we rested all day; aching in every limb and stiff from our heavy journey in the mountains. I felt rather poorly with it; but a good night's rest in the beautiful clean sheets and pillows we can appreciate so, after Asiatic rugs, set all right; and this morning I was up at six, and we breakfasted and packed in time to be on the road at a quarter before eight, for Bashketchet, the village in which Prince H, is exiled. It is a long way, though but little on the map: eighty-five versts, much of which is over downs with no road." Prince Hilkoff, a follower of Tolstoy, lived in a tiny cottage in this Doukhabor village, with his wife and two children. John and Joseph were looked after by a Doukhabor housewife in a larger cottage, next door. "We send him word of our arrival: in a short time he comes in: a man of say five and thirty, dressed in a dark brown tunic of coarse woollen.... He wears a pince-nez, and is very gentlemanly in bearing; indeed it would be impossible to take him for a peasant, though he identifies himself with the peasants in every way he can. At the moment of our arrival he was carrying a burden of firewood.... Princess H. is a pleasant-looking woman of thirty to thirty-six years - oval face, very black hair and eyes... All the people look up to him (Prince H.) almost as an angel. They bring him bread, and potatoes, and flour, and fruit, and everything they have, as much as he needs; and he talks to them in a way to open their eyes to many things, and he tends them in their sickness.

In the morning the good woman of the house baked us some fresh hot cakes for breakfast, and Prince H. brought us a beautiful jug of milk. The meal well over, we started to walk (J.J.N., Prince H. and I) in advance of the horses, over the deep snow.... it was hard to part when the moment came that we must do so ... I felt very closely united with him in spirit."

On their return to Tiflis, the Friends knew that their main work was now completed. They were unable to make their report to the Area Governor as he was ill, so they had to change their plans. They proceeded, instead, to Kutais where they made one more call, and then continued by rail to Poti. Here, they visited an old friend, Wilson Sturge, the British Vice-Consul, and stayed several days. They enjoyed the clean, comfortable beds and the good food, strolls in Wilson Sturge's garden among magnolia and lemon trees, and their first sight of the Black Sea - "mounting the bank, we have the sea almost at our feet - wide, blue and beautiful." Most of all, they enjoyed the companionship of their host, which was equally welcome to him, for his position in Poti was a singularly lonely one.

Making their very last call back in Tiflis, they found the Governor recovered and ready to receive their report. Then they finally left the city to start their homeward journey, taking the railway to Batum, then sailing across the Black Sea to Sevastopol and there made their way to St. Petersburg.

Writing to Elizabeth on the 11th of March from St. Petersburg, "Even yet the tired feeling has not quite gone from either of us, the result in total of our long journey in the 'Zakafkaz'. I dare say this counts for something - perhaps too much - in my dull mental state: for I feel a good deal cast down in the realization of the cruelty and injustice that so largely reign all around us; though I do not know that there is any fresh cause for it." Presumably, the delay of three weeks in St. Petersburg was caused by difficulties in making appointments to report to Ministers and officials, but of these we have no record. We do know that John and Joseph wrote a full report to the Czar, assuring him that he had no more loyal subjects than the Stundists. It is significant to note that John's son, John Earnshaw Bellows, writing of his father, forty years later, says, "A competent observer stated that this visit had had a permanent influence on the attitude of the Czar's Government".

John wrote in his last letter from St. Petersburg, "It is with very mingled feelings that I bid farewell to the city that has played so eventful a part of my life: of delight at the nearing home again: of thankfulness for the help we have had from above: of gratitude and love to the many dear friends who have done all in their power to show their sympathy with us: of sadness that my own share in the work is weak and unsatisfactory: so much so that I could wish to bury it for ever out of my memory, and only to retain the recollection of the friends we have made, and the interesting spots we have travelled in, independently of the occasion of the journey".

They reached London on April 6th, 1893, and gave their report to Meeting for Sufferings* which was accepted with satisfaction.

---

* The Meeting for Sufferings is the Standing Committee of Society of Friends, which meets regularly between the Annual Yearly Meetings.

CHAPTER VIII

Tolstoy and the Doukhabors

ONE OF JOHN'S most valued memories of his time in Russia was his first visit to Count Leo Tolstoy. On this occasion he was accompanied by Joseph Neave and the interpreter, Herman Fast. He wrote of this to Elizabeth, "I do not know what began it - but some question arose about Friends' non-use of 'ordinances', when Fast stated that water baptism was commanded in Scripture, and that all the Scripture was inspired, citing Paul's word to Timothy in proof. Both Count Tolstoy and I combated his position, and the conversation became very earnest and touching..... When I put the Friends' doctrine of Universal and Saving Light before them both, they were both greatly impressed by it.... Count Tolstoy put with admirable force the poorness of the foundation that the letter of Scripture is our guide and not the revelation of God direct to the soul, pointing out that if that were true, then the clever and the learned men would know the most of the things of God instead of the simple and the pure in heart.... If you go by the letter, you will end by having sects without end: but if you are led by the Spirit, it will bring you into one-ness with God. Yes - I *am* glad you have said what you did: I feel - what do you say for it - ? 'Unity,' I suggested. 'Yes, unity. I feel unity with you.'

He persuaded us to stay and take lunch as the time was close at hand. We went downstairs to a dining room leading out of the entrance hall, where most of the family were seated at a table..... 'I will walk back with you to your hotel' Count Tolstoy had said, and now, putting on his peasant's sheepskin coat and fur cap, and taking his staff, we started. The cold was sharp, our moustaches

Hotel d'Angleterre, St Petersburg – John Bellows, 1893 or 94

and beards freezing hard: but I got very warm walking. He told me that to find men dead from cold is not uncommon: though '*vodky*' often has something to do with this.

Count Tolstoy is too continually in earnest to smile often. I only heard him laugh once, and that was when, looking up at some names on the signs, I said, 'I wish your Russian words were not so long. If you would cut them in three I believe I could swallow them and digest them - but now I can do neither.' He seemed tickled, and laughed quite a merry little laugh."

When John returned from the Caucasus six months later, he travelled to Moscow to see Tolstoy, this time on his own. Writing home he says,

"Three or four visits have filled up the time, but by far the larger part of it has been spent at Count Tolstoy's. There are some things in which we see eye to eye; and others that I know to a certainty he is mistaken in, and which I would give much to open his eyes to.

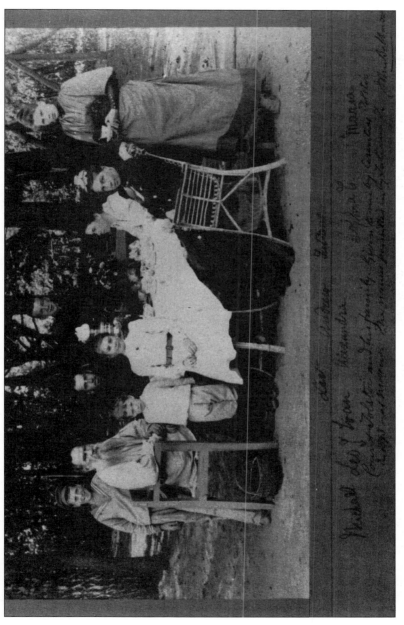

*Left to right: Michael, **COUNT TOLSTOY**, Ivan, Liv, Alexandra, Andrew, Tatiana, **COUNTESS TOLSTOY**, Maria.*
'Count Tolstoy and his family. Given to me by Countess Tolstoy in 1893 – at Moscow.
The names pencilled in by Tatiana T.' – John Bellows

To-day, besides the conversation at his own house, he accompanied me for many miles over Moscow on foot and in the trams."

This part of the visit is described, two years later, by John in a letter to his American friend Senator Hoar. Discussing the Doukhabors, the pacifist sect who had also adopted Tolstoy's teaching, viz. that *all* Government is abhorrent to the Spirit of Christianity, John writes that he and Tolstoy could find no common basis to argue from.

"He has an idea that civilisation, which admits of so many existing evils, is itself the cause of evil, and so would do away with it. Of course he is inconsistent, just as a man would necessarily be who would do away with gravitation. Thus, he resorts to the press constantly, to spread his opinions; but how he could have type-founding and paper-making, etc. etc., without even a very advanced stage of civilisation, passes my comprehension!.... I don't know why I should run on with this gossip, but Tolstoy is so remarkable a man that I believe thou wilt excuse me for doing so. He is narrow-minded in some directions (as we all are, inherently!) and to see something outside of Russia would tend to broaden his views on the real effects of civilisation as distinguished from some of its diseases!"

John's letter continues,

"After lunch this morning, before we started on this round, he (Tolstoy) took a nap, as is his custom. A friend of his, who seems a very thoughtful earnest man, and one of his daughters (Countess Mary Tolstoy) remained at table, asking me about Friends' doctrines. They were deeply interested..... She asked if I believed in the Divinity of Christ. I said, 'I do believe in it: but I do not think it would be of any benefit to thee to force thyself into it, or into any other belief.... The great thing is for all of us to be faithful to the light we already have. That will lead us to all truth..... Presently the two youngest children came in.... Little Ivan is five: his sister Alexandra, a most lovely child of eight..... The two little ones dragged me off, at this point, to the nursery, to shew me their toys and their brother's puppy. 'An English pointer, Mr. Bellows.' 'What is his name?' 'O, he has not got a name yet. You see it is - a little girl - and my brother would rather have a little *boy*: so it will be changed.' 'I think Mr. Bellows will be tired with your taking him about so,' said their sister Mary, coming into the nursery - adding some suggestion about shewing me to her brother's room, if I wished some rest. I declared that I would rather play with the little ones: but Ivan dragged me to a couch - and pushing my head towards the pillow, said 'Repose. Now you can-repose-yourself' but I was to go on, *while* I reposed myself, telling them stories about dogs, *bien entendue*. My heart fairly ached, in the vivid remembrance of our own Jack and Dorothy, as these two little things stood in the porch shouting 'Good-bye!' after me - and promising to come to Upton to play with my children..: 'Your wife will not like you to come back looking so thin,' said Count Tolstoy, this evening, as he was bidding me farewell. You must tell her that you are not feeding yourself enough on this journey: and that if you had stayed with us, we would have looked after you better than you are doing yourself.

As we left the house, Mary Tolstoy slipped on her outdoor wraps and went on before us. Three hours after, when her father and I reached the hotel, I found a little parcel of toys for our children."

Countess Tolstoy had asked if she could send presents to the children (she was somewhat put out when John told her that there were nine) and among the gifts was a little box of birchwood which had held her cold cream: this, in due course, was given to Lucy.

After writing to Tolstoy, on his return to England, John received the following from Yasnaya Polyana dated 14 May 1893.

"Dear Friend, I received your letter from 12 April only just now. I like very much your ideas about not letting our own will go before the will of God and I make it always my chiefest endeavour to discern between the two.

It always was my rule to undertake something, only when I can not do otherwise. So it is with my book that I am publishing now. I am only ashamed that I did not say all what I try to say in this book long time before.

I was very glad to hear that you came safely home and I hope that you are getting stout now. Hilkoff and other exiles wrote to me about you. Your visit did them much good.

> With true love,
> Yours truly L. Tolstoy."

In October 1895, John received another letter from Tolstoy, referring to a gift of ninety-two roubles John had sent him. Tolstoy replied, "I will send it to Tchertkoff who will forward it to its destination. I am sorry that Tchertkoff addressed himself through you to the Society of Friends, and I will avow it to you, that it is very disagreeable to me that I have something to do with this matter. If I thought that it is good for a Christian to have money at his disposal and that good could be done by money, I would have kept my fortune and would help people by my money. But as I think that a Christian ought not to have any property and that it is impossible to do any good through money, I can never ask for money, not for me not for anybody else. If people find it right as you do to give their money to other men and will do it through me, as they did in the time of famine, I will do as they wish, but I would rather not have anything to do with money matters, which are always full of sin.... Excuse me for saying all this, but I prefer to be sincere with you because I like and esteem you very much, and have retained from our intercourse the most kind remembrance.

You have heard I think of the persecution of the Duchobori that is going on in the Caucasus. I have sent correspondence about it to my friend Mr. John Kenworthy (London) and it will, I hope, appear very soon in the English papers.

With best love, your friend

Leo Tolstoy."*

Here, Tolstoy refers to disturbances in Tiflis, where a group of Doukhabors had publicly burned their weapons: their exiled leader, Peter Verigin, had re-kindled their enthusiasm for pacifism, and groups had gathered in Kars, Elisabethpol and Tiflis for a religious protest against the bearing of arms. Only in Tiflis did this cause trouble, when the Cossacks were called out to deal with the Doukhabors and had over-reacted; they killed four people, carried off the leaders to prison, ransacked the nearby settlement and raped the women.

Tolstoy's letter to *The Times* appeared on 23rd October - (the day after his letter to John was posted) - and was entitled "The Persecution of Christians in Russia in 1895". Several Friends, on

---

* Elizabeth Bellows noted "The style of the original has been retained" suggesting this is a translation.

reading this letter, were upset and felt that some action should be taken, but, despite further reports direct from Russia, in *The Times* and *The Daily Chronicle*, no steps were taken to give aid.

Vladimir Tchertkoff, Tolstoy's close friend, had been exiled and was living in England. He was in contact with Friends, and kept them informed of developments in Russia. When he wrote to them again in July 1897, the plight of the Doukhabors had deteriorated. The Czar Nicholas II had tried to mediate with them, offering to return their lands and other privileges, if they would submit to conscription (which they had done in the recent past), but the majority of the Doukhabors were intransigent; life was made increasingly difficult for them and as a result of the civil authority's policy of virtual starvation and extermination, some one thousand members of the sect, living in their mountain settlement, had died.

This time, a new committee of Friends was formed, and John Bellows appointed the Clerk. Again, more appeals were made to the Czar for the Doukhabors to be allowed to emigrate, and, early in April 1898, permission was, at last, granted.

The Relief Committee realised that the task ahead of them was too great for them to tackle without the backing of the whole Society; and, on April 25th, John wrote to Thomas Hodgkin, an eminent member of the Society, "As the Emperor of Russia has now granted permission for the Doukhobortsi to emigrate, in response to their own petition and that of our Meeting for Sufferings, it will be needful to make an appeal to Friends to help these poor people to a new settlement; and I have thought it would enable some Friends the better to grasp the whole position and to realize the claim the Doukhobortsi have on their sympathy, if I were to describe ... two or three Russians who have been their principal helpers.... When Vladimir Tchertkoff got to know of the terrible sufferings of the Doukhobortsi - for their refusal to inflict suffering on others - he took up their cause with all his power, (appealing to Russians of all ranks and positions) and also writing to the English press to ask the sympathy of thoughtful people on their behalf. For this he was ordered into banishment from the Empire. He came to England, and is now living at Purleigh, in a small farm-house, which has been a refuge to several others who have been driven from their homes since his arrival...." His letter goes on to describe two other exiles in the Purleigh farm-house; then he ends his letter thus, "This is a long letter, but I have felt bound to put enough of the story of these men before Friends to show who and what they are who have been raised to carry on that help ... and I feel confident that the Society of Friends will do its part in this emergency, and gladly do it."

The Relief Committee was given the support needed, and were allowed to appeal to Friends in America. However, Tchertkoff was again writing to Friends, in July, to impress on them the urgency of the Doukhabors's needs.

Where were they to go? Canada and Cyprus were considered the best options, out of some ten possible states willing to help the exiles; in the end, Cyprus was chosen. The Committee, with the co-operation of The Cyprus Company, published a plan for re-settlement, suggesting the purchase of two farms at Pergamo and Athalassia, with 1,570 acres of land. The Colonial Secretary, Joseph Chamberlain, and the High Commissioner for Cyprus approved, but insisted that the Committee raised funds, at £20 per head, for transport and the maintenance of the emigrants. The Committee, no doubt, was appalled at what it had taken on, but its members were dedicated and determined to help as many Doukhabors as possible.

Somehow, with the help of Tchertkoff and generous sympathis-ers, the enormous sum of £22,000 was raised by the Committee. A formal letter of acceptance was sent to the Colonial Office, and eleven hundred Doukhabors were given permission to embark from Batum.

Further arrangements had to be made to pay the expenses of the organisers to receive the Doukhabor groups when they arrived in Larnaka. Fortunately, one of the guarantors, George Cadbury, offered to cover these extra expenses, and Wilson Sturge, whom John had met in Poti some years earlier, was considered to be an excellent choice for this work.

Unfortunately, the Doukhabors acted precipitously by chartering their own ship. They sailed from Batum and arrived in Larnaka before provision had been made for them, and Wilson Sturge had not yet arrived! The Cypriot authorities put up tents, and coped with the emergency, but the site chosen was damp and malaria broke out. When Wilson Sturge landed in Cyprus, he had to deal with sickness and families disturbed by their new environment "with a not inconsiderable will of their own". He was helped by a few voluntary workers, including two Russian nurses, Prince Hilkoff and John's own son, Willie.

In John's next letter to Joseph Neave (now in Australia again) dated 27.10.98, he writes, ".... The Canadian Government, on behalf of the Doukhabors, promise a very large grant of land, with advance of seeds and implements, and several other privileges. The cost, even with all this help, for a large number will be of course very great, and with eleven hundred people to feed and find land for in Cyprus, it will be impossible for our Committee to undertake more.... Count Tolstoy is very earnest to go on with the emigration nevertheless, and he has undertaken to write some tales and sell the copyright for the benefit of the Doukhabors, though he has never done such a thing before. Count Tolstoy himself could add £3,000, and his friend V. Tchertkoff about £700. Roundly speaking they expected the cost of transit from Batum to Quebec, and then on by rail, to be about £11,000; and we decided to make them a grant in aid of the balance..... Prince Hilkoff is now away in the far-west of the Dominion looking out for land, a first large tract which was agreed upon by the Government, not being suitable for some reason."

In a further letter to Joseph (Jan. 1899), John says, "With regard to the Doukhabors, at the time I write a company of them are on the Atlantic - perhaps half-way across to Halifax - en route for a tract of land granted them by the Canadian Government..... We now find it needful to re-emigrate the Cyprus company at an early date. It is a weighty undertaking to look forward to; but the way will doubtless be made plain when the right time for it comes".

John's son, Willie, already in Cyprus, accompanied the first group of exiles to Halifax, Nova Scotia. At least 5,000 Doukhabors were settled in Western Canada at this time: eventually the total figure was over 7,000.

In August, 1899, in a letter to Joseph Elkinton of Philadelphia, John writes, "It is a great matter to get the information our son is able to give us about the Doukhabor settlement; for our work as a committee is, I think, by no means near its end yet. We have difficult matters to arrange in Cyprus about the land and buildings, getting the crop sold, etc. - and then in Canada there is the claim of over $5,000 for the quarantine of the last arrivals from Kars, etc.".

Joseph Elkinton, nearly seventy years old, proved to be a tower of strength. He, and other American and Canadian Friends did much to ameliorate the harsh conditions in which the exiles were living, especially during their first years of settlement.

In December 1899, the matter of the one hundred and ten leading Doukhabors, still exiled in Russia and not allowed to emigrate, was brought before the Committee. John Bellows and Edmund W. Brooks were appointed to go to Russia with a petition to the Czar, asking that these exiles might be allowed to join their fellow Doukhabors in Canada. The two Friends were well aware that their mission was going to be a difficult one.

John wrote home from St. Petersburg on 23rd December, ten days after his arrival, "We have done our very best; but it seems that success must not follow our efforts at present. It may come later; but the future is hid from us."

On returning home, he wrote to Joseph Elkinton, "As Count Tolstoy has all along been so deeply interested in this migration of the Doukhabors, and feels so earnestly for the Siberian exiles, we arranged to go over to Moscow to see him. It is a journey by night, of thirteen hours.... We dined and spent the evening with Count Tolstoy and his family, and with one or two of their friends.... Our welcome was warm by every one of the family..... I have been unable to approve of some of Tolstoy's views, or of things he has written: and yet in sitting down by his side I felt the same deep and precious unity of spirit with him which I experienced at out last visit.... Count Tolstoy was earnest that we should leave no possible stone unturned on this errand".

John wrote to Joseph Neave in September 1900, "Thou wilt, I dare say, have followed with interest the account of the visit of Jonathan Rhoads and Joseph Elkinton to the Doukhabor colonies. One item in it was expecially cheering - that a letter has arrived from one of the exiles in Siberia ... in which he says that the officials have informed them that twelve of their number will be at once freed .... we hear the Emperor has stopped the further transportation of Stundists to the Caucasus."

Sometime in 1901, the Relief Committee received £150 from the publication in England of Tolstoy's novel, "Resurrection". Countess Tolstoy had begged Leo not to publish the book at all, but their son Sergei had brought the book to England, on his father's behalf, a year or so earlier, because, being banned in Russia, Tolstoy hoped that it might be translated and published in England. It is likely that John had never read any of Tolstoy's writings, and when he realised its subject was prostitution, he wrote a 'long and earnest' letter to Tolstoy, returning the money. Tolstoy's friend who had helped in the translation, attended the meeting of the Relief Committee to defend Tolstoy's point of view, but the Committee members supported John, and refunded the £150 to him.

Tolstoy's reply, many months later, read, "Dear Friend, I received your letter and meant to answer it; but the last two months I have been so weak that I could not do it, so you must excuse my long silence.

I read your letter twice and considered the matter as well as I could, and could not arrive at a definite solution of the question. You may be right, but I think not for every person which will read the book. It can have a bad influence over persons who will read not the whole book and not take in the sense of it. It might also have quite the opposite influence so as it was intended to. All I can say in my defence is, that when I read a book, the chief interest for me is the Weltanschauung des Autors, what he likes and what he hates. And I hope that the reader which will read my book with the same view will find out what the author likes or dislikes and will be influenced with the sentiments of the author, and I can say when I wrote the book I abhorred with all my heart the lust, and to express the abhorrence was one of the chief aims of the book.

If I have failed in it I am very sorry, and I am pleading guilty if I was so inconsiderate in the scene of which you write that I could have produced such a bad impression on your mind.

I think that we will be judged by our conscience and by God, not for the results of our deeds which we cannot know, but for our intentions, and I hope that my intentions were not bad.

Yours truly,

Leo Tolstoy"

That was their last communication: John died six months later.

The Doukhabors found it difficult to settle in Canada: they had been led to believe (from Tolstoy's teaching) that all government was wrong. They refused to register births, marriages and deaths, or to comply with Government regulations in the registration of land, at first. In time, with the help of tolerant Canadian officials and of American and Canadian sympathisers, they adapted to their new life, and many became successful farmers.

One of the Bellows' children, Hannah, told her father that, as soon as she had graduated from Westfield College, she hoped to go out to Manitoba to teach a group of Doukhabor children. She followed Helen Morland, who returned to England in 1903 to be married, and Hannah was joined by Jessie Ashby Wood. The two teachers lived in a log-cabin, adjoining the house of a prosperous Scottish farmer, named Buchanan.

They walked a mile and a half to the school, which, at first, was a tent, then later a house built by the Doukhabors. About 25 children came to the school, mostly boys. Each day, the children kept a look-out for Hannah and Jessie as they passed, joining the group, one by one, so that when they arrived at the school house, the whole school was with them.

Five years later, Hannah and her brother, Willie, were invited by Vladimir Tchertkoff to stay with his family now living in Russia. His home was very near Yasnaya Polyana, and the high spot of their stay was an invitation to visit the Tolstoy family. Of this Hannah wrote,

"Before dinner, I was taken to see him, ill in bed, but vigorous and able to talk at some length. He had that charming gift of making you feel you were just the one person he wanted to talk to at the time. He spoke English at first, then said he hoped I would not mind if he spoke Russian, as 'I forget my English since I am ill.' He spoke of father and their mutual affection; of the Doukhabors, and what did I think of them? and of our host and hostess.

After dinner I had a talk with Countess Tolstoy in the dining room, a large room with two grand pianos and several family portraits by famous artists. She said she did not regard us as strangers, for they knew and loved my father.

When I came down after seeing Tolstoy, a daughter-in-law, Countess Sophie said to me "Well, and what did you think of him?" I said, 'I did like him so much.' "Yes," she replied, "You know we all love him but we are not allowed to see him. You are very privileged."

Hannah Bellows (second left) in Manitoba, Canada, 1903, with Mr and Mrs Buchanan

CHAPTER IX

Letters, Bulgaria, Peace Conference

THREE MONTHS after John had returned from the Caucasus, he took his family for a month's holiday in Devon.

Writing to John Soper, a Gloucester friend, he says, "In less than a week I expect we shall be back in the usual groove at Gloucester, and to-day we have chartered this vessel for our last sail south: for we are bound for Dartmouth. It is a sunny morning, with a blue sky flecked with white clouds, and a tiny-rippled sea.... the ship is four tons burden, fitted with a seat all round the stern-sheets, in which the whole of my family, except Max and Willie, are variously occupied: Dorothy and Lucy in sailing boats astern, and admiring the seaworthy qualities which enable such small craft to progress either on the water or below it - on an even keel, or capsized, as the case may be. My wife, who ought to have taken precedence in the category, is calmly employed in knitting. Marian and Jack are employed as I am, in letter-writing: Jack's epistle being to Max, and, I suspect, descriptive of the voyage. Kitty, who is always a practical person, is at the helm, obedient to the hints 'Port', 'Starboard' or 'Steady', which drop at intervals from the boatman. Philip is engaged in a general prowl over the ship; now climbing the mast, to his mother's apprehension, and anon, without re-assuring her leaning over the bows to a degree that raises the question of his being able to swim, which he assures her he *can* do."

That John was able to leave his business for another month, after his recent six months' absence, indicates that "John Bellows, Printer" was in good heart, still expanding and under competent

Bellows family: early 1890's

*Back row (left to right): Willie, Philip, Lucy, **JOHN**, Marian, Kitty*

*Front row: Jack, **ELIZABETH**, Dorothy, Max, Hannah*

management. John kept a weather eye on the business. His reputation was of a fair and considerate employer, to whom his workers could take their personal problems.

He introduced a system of bonuses on employees' savings, which was especially popular with those who had given long service. He also welcomed and put into operation the French Government system of *boursiers à l'étranger*, whereby certain French students were given one or two years' experience in foreign business methods; and, in a letter to his friend, Professor Bonet-Maury, who was a member of the selection Committee, he wrote, "I have no hesitation then, in believing that if it were possible very largely to extend this excellent system among the nations of Europe, of letting the young men of one country dwell for awhile among the people of another land, it would be a powerful means of lessening these misconceptions and mistaken ideas about one another, which leads on to war ......"

On another occasion he wrote to Professor Bonet-Maury, "Wilt thou accept my best thanks for the copy of *Le Congres des Religions à Chicago* which has reached me this morning. The first part at which I open (after the kind inscription inside the cover) is page 104 (China) Lao Tse, Confucius and Mencius, as far as they are accessible to us in English; Professor Legge of Oxford, being the Sinologue to whom we are most in debt for this literature. I shall not soon forget a delightful half hour or more that I had at his house, when he gave me a description of a visit he paid, before leaving China, to Confucius' country ..... Professor Legge has a 'rubbing' of the tombstone of Confucius that he made when on the visit referred to. It may be about 70 or 80 cm by 45 cm. At the head is the likeness of Confucius himself, and below, arranged in a *carré*, are his four principal disciples, Mencius and Tseng being the upper two.

Now, in the figures of these men there are square caps on their heads, exactly such as are now worn by students at Oxford. I asked Professor Legge whether this was really the fact, that such caps were worn as far back as the time of Confucius. He said, 'That cap has been worn in China for two thousand five hundred years as the sign of a *teacher*!'"

John continued his varied correspondence, which not only expressed his interest in a wide diversity of subjects, but revealed his perceptive concern for those around him.

Senator Hoar (whose forbears came from Gloucester) had been an American friend of Oliver Wendell Holmes, and shared John's interest in archaeology. In his correspondence, he wrote of John's election to the American Antiquarian Society, "I write chiefly to say that I hope you will contribute for us a paper for our next meeting, which will be in October. You can select your own subject. And you may be sure that what is common learning to you will be of great interest to us."

In 1894, he contributed a paper on "The past and the Present in Asia", in which he noted the similarity between the single-headed pick and the three-cornered shovels, used currently in the Cornish tin-mines with those he had seen in traditional use at the Kedabek mines in the Caucasus; these long-hilted shovels were used, also, in Tiflis to clear mud off the cobbled streets.

John wrote to Senator Hoar, to tell him how he had tried out his lecture to an English audience, "I think it will interest thee to know that I tried the effect of the article I have just sent thee a few days ago, upon a company of about seven hundred smiths and working engineers, employees of my old friends, the Tangyes of Birmingham. I did not read the paper to them, but gave them magic-lantern slides of scenery I travelled through in the Caucasus, the town of Tiflis, etc. and showed them the forgings I describe in the paper. I never had a more appreciative audience; for the technical side of the subject suited them peculiarly" (The Tangye brothers, originally from Illogan, had been John's childhood friends in Cornwall).

In 1895, the interest of the Society of Friends was aroused by the arrival of Khama, the Chief of Bechuanaland. He had come to England to plead for the expulsion of intoxicants from his country. Writing to Colonel Carleton of Clevedon, John explains, "A fortnight ago it was my lot to go with another Friend (Edmund Wright Brooks) as a deputation from the Society, to the Colonial Secretary (Joseph Chamberlain) to hand him a memorial praying that Khama might be permitted to still keep alcoholic drink out of his territory. He has fought a hard battle to keep his people from

87

this curse; and it would be sad if the power of the Empire were used to force back such a work.

Joseph Chamberlain was fully in sympathy with the object, though he explained to us some of the difficulties of *entirely* excluding drink from the territory. Still, he has done more than has ever been attempted before, for he not only will not permit any new licences, but he is going to extinguish one in Bathoen's reserve, which Lord Ripon had granted."

The next year, he was again writing to Senator Hoar, "If the day is ever to come when the sword shall be beaten into ploughshare and the nations learn war no more, *someone* must make the beginning? If it falls to the lot of 'Friends' to do this, even if they do not succeed in inducing any large number of their fellow-citizens to follow them they may at least increase the employment of arbitration..... I find it a harder task to overcome my own hasty temper than to advise my neighbour to curb his."

To Elizabeth Putnam of Boston, in somewhat different vein, he writes, "Last summer it was the fortune of my wife and myself to be guests in a house that stands on Chelsea Embankment, overlooking the Carlyle Monument. Turner the artist had lived not far away; and as we looked from our window at the sunrise over the broad shining Thames, it was easy to see where he had gained his idea of mist-effects; for it would be difficult to imagine anything more beautiful in landscape than the white dazzling cloud that linked *something* to *nothing*, and that gently turned the crimson and gold of the water and the bridges and barges in the foreground into half-tones, and then into haze and poetry (and *all* poetry depends upon that which is *in*definite because it leaves play for the fancy!) in the distance."

By now, John was corresponding with Chief Justice Holmes, Oliver's son, another enthusiastic amateur archaeologist. In his letter, he says, "I send with this one or two little things I had put by to hand to thee.... A few *tesserae* from Lydney Park. Close by this spot, where rabbits had thrown them out, are the remains of an important Temple overlooking the mile-wide Severn..... Among the rest are some thin metal letters that had been fastened by pins to the stone facade of the temple - NODENS - probably the name of the god to whom it was erected. Noddyns would be, in Celtic,

88

the Abyss, or Deep - i.e. the God of the Deep. Such temples were also health resorts - and a more lovely spot for the site of such an establishment could hardly be imagined: wooded hills, green lawns and pastures, the lake-like river, and the exquisite lines of blue mountain scenery beyond it, must have tempted many a wealthy Roman and Briton to Lydney."

At the end of 1896, John was asked by the Friends Armenian Relief fund committee (of which he was a member) to travel to Bulgaria to oversee the work being done there. John had now rejoined Friends and, in 1897, became an Elder of Gloucester Meeting, and a member of the Central Committee, Meeting for Sufferings.

On this occasion, Elizabeth accompanied him, together with James Adams, a Friend from Yorkshire, who had been appointed to arrange accommodation and work for the refugees.

John describes this visit in a letter to Chief Justice Holmes, "..... Just about the time of thy leaving England, as thou wilt remember, the whole world was horror stricken at the great massacre of Armenians by the lowest of the Mahometan population of this city of Constantinople. Consequent on this was a flight of many thousand Armenian refugees to all places within easy reach of Turkey, but outside the frontier: more especially to Varna, in Bulgaria, which lies within a couple of days sail of Constantinople......."

The three left London: John and Elizabeth bound for Constantinople and Adams for Varna, but because of floods at Sofia, they were all diverted to Varna, via Bucharest, where, incidentally, John was intrigued to discover that many of its inhabitants spoke an Italian dialect. His letter continues, "Trajan built a wall across from the Danube to Kustendje, which is the Turkish alteration of *Constantia;* and I have no doubt that it was having this wall, then just built, in his mind, that suggested the idea to Hadrian of making one from Newcastle to Carlisle.... Both are about the same length - some 70 miles.

Leaving Bucharest we got late in the evening to Giurgevo, on the Danube; crossing the river next morning in the stinging cold of a Russian winter, the steamer tearing its course through two-inch ice for part of the passage. At Rushchuck - a semi-Turkish town on the other bank - we found the first large gathering of refugees. They are quartered wherever shelter could be got cheaply. Among other places the Relief Committee had rented a Theatre, and lodged fifty families in it .....

At Varna the climate was milder; and well it is for the refugees that it is so. Here again they are quartered all over the town..... Our friend Adams has set to work also, hiring rooms, buying tools and materials, and getting some artisans into employment in their own trades."

The Bulgarian Government had been generous in helping the refugees - they provided bread for the first month and free passage on the railways, so that they might disperse to inland areas rather than overcrowd the coastal towns. Workshops were established in Varna for the making of wood and metal domestic articles and to help those with special skills to use them. John tried, unsuccessfully, to find large knitting needles, used for the coarse cotton foundation of rugs. However, he bought some stout brass and took it to a stove-maker who beat it straight and shaped the ends.

Writing to his daughter, Hannah, he says, "We were both measured for boots this morning by an Armenian shoemaker refugee. He does beautiful work. We started him with leather and tools, and he made the first pair yesterday for James Adams. 'Why don't you *smile*?' said J.A. as he spoke a few cheery words to him in launching the business. 'I have no smiles left,' was the reply. 'I saw my brother torn to pieces in Constantinople by the Turks, when I made my escape, and I cannot smile now.'"

After two weeks in Varna, John and Elizabeth went by sea to Constantinople. There, they heard many stories of the horrors suffered by the Armenians when they contacted the local Relief agencies.

On their way home, John wrote to his children from the Orient Express, describing the Armenian who had cooked for them in Constantinople. "Ovannes - for that is his name - is a little man, with black hair and black eyes, very thin. I gave him my old great coat, which comes down to his heels. In it, and his red fez, he looks fairly like a European Jew. Anyhow, he is on board ship, and if I might venture a guess as to his present whereabouts, it is that he is now leaning over the gunwale of the steamer, shivering amid the

90

isles of the Aegean Sea, in my great coat, sea-sick, and muttering in Armenian 'Oh that I had died by the hand of the Turk, instead of coming to this!' But in a week he will land and get work, as he has a kinsman in Alexandria awaiting him.

He is a very good cook - and when your mother one day admired some dough nuts and asked him for the recipe, he showed her how he had oiled his hand over, and squeezed the paste out of his fist in little balls, into boiling fat. A queer expression passed over her face as she realised the process, and though Ovannes went away delighted, and prepared to make enormous numbers of the nuts, I have not noticed your mother asking for any more."

In June 1899, he wrote to William Holland, of Norquay, Manitoba, to whom he owed a letter, "As for correspondence, since my friend Tchertkoff writes me that he has by him ninety-five unanswered letters up till this day week, I take comfort on the principle of our Jack, who, when a little boy, came home aglow with excitement from school to tell his mother that 'there's a prize at our school for the best boy!' 'And who has got it?' asked my wife, with evident hope in her eye. 'Oh *nobody* hasn't got it, because there is no best boy. We are all as bad as each other - only I'm not the *worst*!'"

The letter continues, "I have had to be three times in London during two weeks, chiefly on account of the 'Yearly Meeting' of Friends there. On the 24th ult. they decided to send an address to the President of the Peace Conference at the Hague. The draft of this document was adopted on the forenoon of the 25th., and six persons chosen to take it over to Holland, of which I was one........ At 8.30 we were in the train to Harwich and the Hook of Holland; and at seven next morning we were at the Hague...... a little before six our party walked quietly to the Doelon, to our appointment..... In a few moments we were shown into the President's room. A very gentle old man, with silver hair and a sweet sorrowful smile that won one's heart, received us with a warm shake of the hand: a few preliminary words; and then we asked if we might be permitted to read the address to him".

This peace conference had been called by Czar Nicholas II and was presided over by a Russian; all the great powers were represented, the United States' envoy being Andrew White. He had been the American Ambassador in St. Petersburg and had met John there. In his autobiography, he wrote of the delegates, "Best of all, by far, was John Bellows of Gloucester, our old Quaker friend at St. Petersburg whom I was exceedingly glad to take by the hand: he, at least, is a thoroughly good man - sincere, honest, earnest and blessed with good sense."

When John left the Hague, he travelled to Sweden for a brief visit to take up the cause of Norwegian conscientious objectors.

Back at home, he wrote again to William Holland about visits made to his much-loved Forest of Dean. (Possibly William was related to the Colonel Holland with whom John had written the guide, *A Week's Holiday in the Forest of Dean* published in 1881.) "A number of unforeseen things have thrown my work into arrear: the last being a somewhat sudden visit of Senator Hoar, of Massachusetts, who is now for the sixth time in England. He wanted to see some of the older oak trees in the Forest of Dean; and before I was aware of it, he had engaged a carriage and pair and driven over from Malvern to beg me to accompany him. So the following morning we drove to Lydney, calling on Sir James Campbell (the late Deputy Surveyor of the Forest) from whom we obtained much curious information about oak planting....... From Lydney we drove to Whitemead Park ..... saw the very large oak .... in Churchill enclosure 21 ft. 7 ins. circumference 6 ft. up, and then drove on in the moonlight to Speech House."

At the end of 1899, John contributed a paper on "The Forest of Dean" to the American Antiquarian Society and Senator Hoar sent him a copy of The Society's proceedings, telling him that, "The whole paper gave great pleasure to the Society. Your account of the working of that mighty machine, a Roman army, was specially interesting. Waldo Emerson once said of William Ellery Channing that he could read into a hymn a sense that nobody else who read it could ever find there. You have certainly put into Statius a vigour and lofty stroke of poetry which it is a little difficult to find there!"

CHAPTER X

The Boer War

AT THE BEGINNING of January, 1900 John was travelling by train from Swindon to Gloucester, when he got into conversation with two soldiers who were on embarkation leave for the South African Boer War, and were fearful of saying good-bye to their families. On arriving at Gloucester, John helped them both with their journeys home (one had an eight-mile walk) and promised to write to them.

His first letter, addressed to Private George Roberts and Private Joseph Goodall, South Wales Borderers, included,- "I know myself what it is to be hundreds of miles away from home in a foreign land, when I have been glad of ever such a little kindness from a stranger, but I have had no one to ask help of but God. Only a few weeks ago I was half as far off from here as you will be at the Cape; but in the north of Russia. It was dreadfully cold, and I got a chill one evening that made me feverish, and so bad in a few hours that I was suddenly brought face to face with the chances of death. It looked black enough to have to pass away without a word of farewell to wife or child, and lie under the snow yonder; and so I know exactly what many a soldier has to feel besides his bodily pain, when he comes to die on the field of battle. It may be that one of you may have this to pass through - though with all my heart I hope it will not".

Sadly, one of the men died of Enteric Fever in South Africa, and John did all he could to help his widow and family.

Later, John published his views on the Boer War, which are decribed by Elizabeth in the memoir of her husband, "In the summer of 1900, John Bellows published a pamphlet entitled *The Truth about the Transvaal War* in which he defended the British Government from what he considered unjust attacks upon its policy in South Africa. During a journey to Russia in the previous winter, he had noticed the ignorance of his friends there, on the past history of the Transvaal question; and this led him to enquire into the whole subject more closely. He spent much time and care in the compilation of his pamphlet, in which he showed that the British Government was justified in its contention that the war had been forced upon it. His testimony against war, as the second part of his work would show, was not abandoned; for his conviction was that 'war is wrong: but not alike wrong to all'. The position he took upon the question led him into considerable controversy at the time. The pamphlet had a large issue, and was subsequently translated into French and German, and circulated on the Continent."

This document caused a furore amongst Friends, most of whom supported the Boers, and John became a central figure in the controversy as, seemingly, the only articulate supporter of the British Government's South African policy. In *The Truth about the Transvaal War* he had thoroughly researched the historical background to the war: he was critical of the Boers' failure to give the native population equal civil rights to those of the Boers themselves (as was British policy), and he showed that most of the black Africans preferred to be under British rule. He also produced evidence that Kruger was persistently untrustworthy and manipulative in his negotiations with the British, and that he had no sincere interest in arbitration. He argued a well-documented case supporting the British Government.

In his pamphlet, he wrote, "Some of the Friends in this land, in well-intentioned zeal against war, have circulated tracts about the Transvaal which they have not first examined with sufficient care: and so have committed themselves unawares to statements which the evidence in these columns* shows to be untrue. Anti-Semitism and ravings against 'Capitalists' are singularly out of harmony with the teachings of a body professing such regard for the history of the Patriarchs, many of whom were Jews, and of whom nearly all who were good for anything were Capitalists and Landowners. How

* Probably referring to letters and articles in *The British Friend*.

94

could Noah have built the Ark, or Joseph have steered Egypt through seven years of famine without Capital

Not every advocacy of peace is true or honest, any more than preaching of the Gospel of Peace was so in New Testament times; but even some good and honest peace-advocates built upon too narrow a basis. Thus they decry 'Patriotism' because the term is often abused by being made a mask for the war spirit....... it is as natural and right for me to love my own country better than any other, as it is that I should care for my own family before all other families. This is the same for every nationality." The last pages of his pamphlet were devoted to his views on pacifism.

On returning from his relief work in Metz, he had expressed his difficulties over pacifism to his friend Max Müller. He repeated them in a letter written to Gamaliel Milner, of Mary-de-Crypt Rectory in Gloucester, "I thank thee for thy letter, with nearly every word of which I am in personal agreement. I say personally, because I feel that my real conviction is short of the highest standard in this matter of war. That is, it is a matter rather of spiritual growth, or state, than of mere theory....... Individually I feel I dare under no circumstances assist in any way in military matters, even if the refusal involved death. At the same time I am fully persuaded that numbers of excellent men are not shown this as *their* duty: and for them war is not *per se*, a sin."

His actions were felt to be disloyal to the cause of pacifism by the many Friends who may have suffered by their conscientious objection to war, and their pro-Boer convictions, during a period of jingoistic fervour. John had little interest in politics as such: Elizabeth wrote that he seldom used his vote or showed interest in party politics. However, he did embrace specific causes where he felt that justice or truth were at stake.

A certain attack by notable Friends caused him to retaliate with an angry and bitter reply to his critics, which was most untypical of his writings. A criticism levelled against John had been that he had made serious errors of judgment in the past. In a leaflet, issued in 1900, he had written, "Nearly forty years ago I made two serious mistakes - one in attacking John Bright, and the other in imagining that the Southern States of America were struggling for their proper rights. I have long been sorry for these mistakes, and have said so."

He was particularly upset by what his old friend, Frederick Sessions, had written. Frederick was much respected by Gloucester Friends, and there is little doubt that they, especially, were dismayed by John's controversial stance. Nevertheless, when John died eighteen months later, his Obituary in the *Gloucester Journal* was accompanied by a generous Appreciation of him by Frederick Sessions, touching on their differences, but emphasising their mutual affection and respect.

Frederick Sessions

CHAPTER XI

The Last Journey, the USA, Harvard,
Illness and Death

"THY LITTLE NOTE is especially a pleasure to me on reaching this seventieth year of my life: an age I should have looked upon as dismaying, from a distance, but not in the least so on closer sight of it," wrote John to Hannah after his birthday on 18th January 1901. This was only a few months after his defence of his position over the Boer War (which must have been deeply disturbing to him).

Quite surprisingly, he was asked to speak on Peace at Westminster Meeting, in February 1901. He wrote out his speech reiterating his views on pacifism but did not attend, perhaps because of his distaste for public speaking.

In March 1901 he was among a number of Quaker delegates appointed by the Society of Friends to convey an address at Buckingham Palace to King Edward the Seventh on his accession to the throne. Here he describes this occasion in a letter to his son Philip in Philadelphia, "... A buzz of conversation behind us gets a little too loud for etiquette, and an officer in front gives a gentle 'sh'. This is not for the Friends, however, but for Lord Roberts and a little knot of officers just behind us who are waiting their turn for some other deputation. Then the door opens and we all move forward between the lines of Life Guards, to the front of the throne. The King, seated on it, is dressed in scarlet; the Duke of Cornwall and York, on his left, standing, is dressed in black with many stars and insignia, and a gentleman I cannot identify stands on the right of the throne. On either hand of these stand officers and Life

Guards. Caleb Kemp steps slightly in advance, and reads - 'May it please the King' and so on."

Philip, now settled in America and working as an engineer, was an additional factor in John and Elizabeth's decison to accept at last the offers of hospitality they had received from American friends (both Quaker and non-Quaker).

They embarked from England in early May 1901 and first visited their friends, Joseph and Melinda Elkinton living in Philadelphia. Joseph had been particularly helpful to the Doukhabor communities in Manitoba: he and many of the Philadelphian Friends had assisted in settling the immigrants when they had first arrived in Canada.

In one of the many letters to their children, John wrote of their journey South, "It was an interesting run (from New York to Philadelphia) some of the scenery very much reminding one of Belgium .... I need hardly say how warm a welcome we had from the house-

John and Elizabeth on board ship, bound for the USA 1901

hold. Invitations began to pour in on us. Joshua L. Bailey has called and arranged for us to be at his house on Fifth-day next; and we go this afternoon to William Evans's at Moorestown, to stay over to-morrow".

They were entertained by many local Friends, particularly in Moorestown; they were shown round the City, and, one day, taken by Thomas Elkinton to Fairmount Park in a barouche. Unfortunately the summer of 1901 was exceptionally hot, even for America, and John was troubled by difficulty in breathing and by exhaustion: their plans had to be altered, and he and Elizabeth were advised to spend a few days at Niagara which was thought to be cooler. "We got here between twelve and one at night, and were taken to the Cataract Hotel. The journey had been a long one: part of it - a large part - through the beautiful scenery Willie advised us not to miss. Two points especially struck us. Glen Summit, 2,000 feet above the sea, in the midst of wooded hills stretching away to an immense distance ..... the second very beautiful feature was the Seneca Lake by sunset. It is thirty-seven miles long - say as far as from Bristol to Gloucester - and about as wide as Windermere. Here and there lovely gorges and woods run down to it; and much of the land on the side on which the rail runs is cultivated for fruit - peaches, grapes, etc. ...It was half-past ten, nearly, when we reached Buffalo City, where we waited an hour or more for the train to Niagara Falls. ...To get below them, on the little steamer, is the best way to form an idea of their scale..... to look up one hundred and sixty feet and see the mighty roll-over of the mass of emerald green water against the sky-line of blue, a thousand feet wide, and watch it always plunging down into a vast sea of cloud that hides the river where it strikes, and have all the hearing filled with the hiss and boom and thunder of it, nearly stuns the imagination."

From Niagara they travelled to Worcester, Mass. to stay with Senator George Hoar and his wife, Ruth. "Everything here is so full of interest that it is hard to keep pace with the new thoughts suggested by each place.... Yesterday we had a delightful excursion to the neighbouring towns of Clinton and Lancaster, going to the first on a trolley car, some half-dozen miles through a delightful country of hills and woods, past the new lake that is being made for the larger supply of Boston with water.... This morning Senator Hoar took me to Boston: your Mother coming on later with our hostess to join us at the Union Club."

The day in Boston was memorable for John and Elizabeth - they were taken to the State House, the Assembly and the Senate. They met the Secretary of State, called the State Governor, and lunched in the Union Club with Chief Justice Holmes and other notable Americans.

"After lunch we joined the ladies, and then Chief Justice Holmes took your Mother and me to his father's old house on the River Charles.... Armstrong Howitt's carving of the city area of

Gloucester - taken from the Tolsey at the time of its being 'torn down' - is built into the mantelpiece of Oliver W. Holmes's room overlooking the water."

The previous day, with many members of the Hoar family, they had visited "The Redemption Rock" near Lake Wachusett, to celebrate a two hundred and twenty-five anniversary. "The Redemption Rock" is a mass of granite, nearly flat, about forty feet by twenty-five, and some twelve feet high, or more, with trees round part of it, and an open field at the back. All clambering on the top, we stood in a group while Senator Hoar graphically told us the story of the capture and redemption of Mary Rowlandson by his Gloucester ancestor.... He and his wife signed the deed, all the rest of us following on with our names, as witnesses. George Hoar now called his grand-nephew forward and made him a present of the property, which he had purchased to preserve it in the family. John Hoar is a bright boy of nine. Taking the deed of gift from the Senator, he said in a clear voice, 'Uncle Frisbie, I will keep this precious deed in memory of John Hoar and of you.'

They were taken to Plymouth to see the spot where the Pilgrim Fathers had landed. Arthur Lord, Secretary of the Pilgrim Society, welcomed them and told them much about the Pilgrim Fathers and showed them the Pilgrim Hall, a museum which held an interesting collection of documents and memorabilia.

In his next letter, dated 27.6.1901, he admitted that "Such a pressure of events has been about us for several days that I hardly know where I dropped the last thread of narrative. On Sixth-day we were taken over the Concord, one of the most beautiful of the New England towns.... We were met at the station by Samuel Hoar, a nephew of Senator Hoar. He drove us to the scene of the battle of Concord, and then to the lovely burial ground of 'Sleepy Hollow' where Emerson, the Thoreaus, Hawthorne, the Alcott family and many of Senator Hoar's family lie interred".

The high spot of the visit is described by John in a letter to William Holland, when he and Elizabeth were taken to Harvard, "Before leaving England I had a letter from Senator Hoar saying that he hoped I could plan to be present at this function (Harvard Commencement) and adding that he thought they might give me a degree! I at once wrote that I did not want to put myself in a false position, that I was not of a calibre to take part in such a festival, and must therefore decline it. Writing to Andrew White (the U.S. Ambassador at Berlin, whom I had known at Petersburg and at the Hague, and who was giving me some introductions for this journey) I told him what I had said about Harvard; but he at once urged me to go there." The letter continues, "Just before the procession formed up on the morning to march to the theatre where the degrees were to be conferred, Senator Hoar came to me and said I had to walk with him (he is the President of the Alumni) at the head of it.... Of course, there was nothing for it but to comply, and so we set out, followed by the Governor of Massachusetts and the German Ambassador, then the Vice-President of the United States (Theodore Roosevelt).

Just before starting, the Chief Marshal told me that when my name was mentioned by President Eliot, I must stand up in my place, but not to speak. We went through a double rank of some thousands of graduates, to the 'Theatre' and on to the platform.... When the honours came, two or three others and myself were recommended by the Board of Overseers as worthy to have conferred upon us the degree of Master of Arts; and so, *nolens volens* I found myself an 'M.A.' of Harvard for my French dictionary and Roman remains essays!"

It was at this ceremony that John and Elizabeth met members of the American branch of the Bellows family, descendants of the John Bellows, who as a boy of twelve had sailed from London in April 1635. One member, Dr. Henry Whitney Bellows, had called on John in Gloucester, England, in the eighteen sixties.

George and Ruth Hoar had intended taking John and Elizabeth to the poet, John Whittier's home in Amesbury, but George Hoar had been "much affected by the heat at the Harvard Commencement" and was unable to make the journey. John amazingly survived the fierce temperatures, so he and Elizabeth went on their own. They stayed in Whittier's house for a few days.... "Ours is the guest chamber, next to the poet's own bedroom. I can touch the ceiling with my hand. Two windows look out on the street, under the elms; another into the garden. The little parlour downstairs, in which Whittier sat and wrote, looks out into this; and he always called it 'the garden room'.... this morning we went to Amesbury

Meeting - a nice little gathering of perhaps forty Friends. Your Mother sat in Whittier's seat." This was their last visit before returning home.

In a letter to George Hoar, from Gloucester, dated 3.8.1901, he explains, "Here we are, back at home again, after our nearly three months' delightful journey in your land, laden like bees with the pollen of practical information about many matters in it, and with the honey of the friendships we have made, and deepened.

Our son, with a friend, ran up from Philadelphia to see us off from New York, which we left with almost the punctuality of a train, to dream our way across the Atlantic on our floating Island, the *Oceanic*: an Island flowing with milk and honey, and producing all the fruits and grains of the temperate zone and the tropics, from Quaker oats to oranges growing ready peeled on forks, coming into our cabin in the morning to entice us out to breakfast.

On that voyage I had planned a round of work suitable to the leisure it affords - letters to friends, essays, dictionary work and more than I can now even recall. But if, on land, the way to ruin is paved with good intentions, at sea these take the form of clouds that disappear by day and leave not a rack behind!"

The return journey from America had been peaceful and John appeared to have benefited from his visit, but the improvement in his health did not last long. Two months later he was writing from his bed ".... laid on the shelf by my illness." His activities were much restricted, but his correspondence continued, though less frequently.

In January 1902, he was writing to Chief Justice Holmes about a new book, *Literary Associations in the English Lakes* by Canon Rawnsley[*], "I had a climb with him two summers ago to a height above Keswick on which a camp commanded the Derwent Valley on the one side, and that leading to Thirlmere and Ambleside on the other ... nowhere in the world is such a variety of mountain forms so inwrought with poetic legend brought into a single landscape. Skiddaw and Blencathra and the Western Cumberland hills on the north, the Borrowdale heights to the south, and the

[*] The Co-founder of the National Trust with Robert Hunter and Octavia Hill.

range of Helvellyn to the east, magnificent in themselves, were all linked with Wordsworth and his compeers".

He wrote rather differently on the same day to George Hoar, whom he had known more intimately, describing his increasing attacks of cardiac asthma, "Yes, I quite hope we may keep up this correspondence, which has been one of the privileges of my life ...I dare say thou canst enter into the experience of a man accustomed to a busy life being thus set aside from it suddenly? It is as if one had been sailing along day after day over a blue sea, and were all at once stranded on a sandbank to watch the tide recede and feel the uncertainty of ever floating again.

"The doctors come with their stethoscopes, and after taking soundings declare that there is nothing organically wrong, that it is all due to nervous exhaustion; and that time and rest may set all right again. Perhaps they may. ....One feature of asthma is the inability to breathe sufficiently while lying down. And after hours of sitting up and leaning forward, in bed, I devised one day a board, on two little stands about fifteen inches high, on which one can lean the forehead (on a small pillow) with a semi-circular gap cut out for the mouth. It is about three feet six inches long, and with it I have had excellent nights of rest!"

Then later, on hearing of Ruth Hoar's illness, he writes "We have been much concerned to learn of thy wife's failure of health at Washington. ...As I write in my room upstairs, I have been wishing she could have such invalid quarters as mine, with all this wide reach of landscape to look out on and with the sound of the breeze coming through the open window, I was going to say in music: but it is something more than music. It comes sweeping through the trees, gathering up tones that are different from different species. The sound in the leafless beeches is sweet, but it is not the same sound as in the foliage of the fir-trees, and so on. ...I can *appre*hend, though I cannot *com*prehend, such an effect from watching the play of the sunlight on the towers in different parts of the landscape. ...thus, there is a lovely Lombardy poplar not far from my window - one that I planted some years ago. At sunrise all the leafless twigs are golden in colour, but near the top there is one branch that stands away from the rest, of course giving a variant note to the wind that sweeps over it. No doubt when the tree was younger, some starling or homeward-bound rook rested on the twig that was not then strong enough to bear his weight, and so he gave the plant this set for all time. I used to think it would be well to cut off this branch for the sake of uniformity; but I could not reach it. Now I would rather have it as it is. And is it not so in life? We are too fearful of divergences."

On reading this one feels that had he not adhered so strictly to his self-denying ban on music and theatre, how readily he would have responded to them. He had, after all, refused to handle reports of music or drama in his printing business. Yet, in his writing, he showed a marked awareness of the sounds of nature such as running water, bird-song and here, the music of the wind in the trees; and whenever it came his way he showed his appreciation of pageantry and spectacle. No doubt this was one of the contradictions in his nature to which he alluded when he wrote, "I cannot add one inch to my stature, nor make myself spiritually anything else but the strange compound of inconsistencies I have been most of my life".

In mid-February he was in touch with Joannin Ardouin, a Parisian friend, "Though I still am ill, and write this *au lit*, I am not without hope that the summer may enable me to get out again. It would be a real pleasure to see thy wife and thyself here. ...It was rather singular that the same mail that brought me thy letter, mentioning Harvard, also brought one from the President of the University asking me to cable a reply whether I could go to Manchester and represent Harvard at the fiftieth anniversary of Owen's College. Of course I have to cable, 'Impossible'."

In these last letters he touches more often on his faith, and here he continues thus to his French friend, "Many people do not go deeper than a creed or belief; but to me, as God is *en rapport* with all that He creates, He is manifested, in varying degree certainly, but still manifested, to every human heart, showing every man what is good and what is evil. And perfectly irrespective of whether one is a Christian, or a Mahometan, or a Jew, or a heathen, every man who forsakes evil and does *right,* draws near to God and is approved of him. Take Confucius as an instance. No one can read his life without being convinced that he was in deed and truth a good man - and what is more, an *extraordinarily* good man: that his goodness was a growth, being much more marked later in life than it was at first."

His final surviving letter was written at the end of February in 1902, "To the Sergeant in charge of the Ordnance Survey of Gloucester" and starts, "I am always glad to be of any help in Roman matters". He goes on to describe the probable course of the *Via Julia*, explaining that the road was named after Julius Frontius, who was both a very able Roman General and a skilled engineer. At the end of his interesting and highly informative letter, he could not conclude

Elizabeth Bellows, 1893

without an analysis of place-names (which may, or may not, have intrigued the Sergeant).

In his personal life there is no doubt that he was profoundly convinced of the presence of God, and communed with Him, daily. He was receptive to the inner promptings which guided his actions, and which led him to undertake any task, regardless of the consequences. The other overwhelming influence was that of his wife, Elizabeth. He was deeply attached to her and relied on her completely, always sharing his problems and decisions with her. It is evident that she was much in love with him. Looking at her photograph, taken when she was fifty years old, she appears amazingly peaceful for a mother who has reared nine children and has weathered the storms that her husband's views and activities had brought upon the family: most particularly those resulting in his temporary alienation from the Society of Friends.

The children were a constant source of pleasure to him; their upbringing seems to have been both disciplined and surprisingly free. Their lives, naturally, took them in different directions, but they all remained in touch with each other, that is with the exception of Philip who settled in the United States. What they retained in common with each other were the memories of a happy and lively childhood, mutual affection - with some inevitable jealousies - and a capacity for enjoying life. Only Max, Willie and Lucy remained Quakers while four of the others became Christian Scientists.

John's letters give an incomplete picture of his many friendships, as, not unnaturally, those kept by his family are from the better known of his correspondents. A remark made by Lord Ducie, who had corresponded with him for over thirty years, often in Norwegian, was that John was so many-sided that no man could be said to know him thoroughly. His son, Jack, (John Earnshaw Bellows) was mainly responsible for preserving the letters. In writing a short centenary tribute to his father, in 1931, Jack comments on the many other friendships that his father had made. There are, for example, his Quaker friends in Gloucester and his local friends in his own village. Jack writes, "By few was he more deeply loved than by his own neighbours in Gloucestershire, where he had won for himself a position of special esteem.... John Bellows used to enjoy meeting the people from his own village and from them he gleaned many interesting details regarding bygone events which he carefully wrote down and preserved. He was so accustomed to giving villagers a lift on his way to and from his business that his horse got into the habit of stopping when it saw them on the road. One of his neighbours was a bed-ridden old man whom he used to visit every Sunday afternoon, accompanied by his big St. Bernard dog. One Sunday, when John Bellows was away from home, the old man was delighted by a visit from the dog alone, and this was repeated each Sunday till his master's return."

The last, though somewhat eulogistic appreciation of John's life and personality is found in a tribute to his memory by the Mayor of Gloucester, Dr. Sidney Hartland, on the 6th January 1903, some eight months after John's death. Lord Ducie, here as the Lord Lieutenant of the County, presented a portrait (by Percy Bigland) on behalf of the subscribers, to hang in the Guildhall. In his speech, Dr. Hartland gives a vivid picture of John's appearance and nature.... "His lean, tall figure, slightly bent, his quaint garb, his bright and earnest eyes, arrested the attention at once. When you got into conversation with him, no matter about what, his quiet manner, his old-world speech and courtesy, his wide knowledge and accurate memory, his readiness to listen, as well as to talk, his kindly witticisms, and his endless store of facts and anecdotes constituted an unbounded charm. Further acquaintance made known a character of the deepest and most solemn convictions, sharply defined beliefs carried out in daily life with punctual and even ritualistic formality, but all controlled and brought into harmony by an over-flowing kindliness, a spontaneous love for his fellow-men that impelled him not merely to avoid offence, but to seek for their highest good ...You had found a unique personality, the impress of which would be an abiding possession... Whether it were the making of a dictionary, or the living of a religion, the advocacy of a policy of state, the pursuit of a scientific enquiry or the earning of his bread, thoroughness was everywhere and at all times much more than a matter of conscience: it was a necessity he could no more escape than he could escape his own soul."

Despite his eminence he remained a modest man of simple tastes; he was unusual in the breadth of his knowledge, his inventiveness and the variety of his achievements. He was, moreover, a man of great spiritual integrity who never proselytised: if he was asked to give help or spiritual advice, he would say, "Be faithful to the light thou has, and thou wilt have more." He was never dull: on the contrary his contemporaries (and his family) relished his company, his humour and his enthusiasms. Above all, his interest was in people: he was an unusually attentive listener, which led him to a perceptive understanding of his fellows.

As Spring returned in 1902, it was evident that John's strength was gradually fading: he was less able to take the occasional drive into the country, and his breathing became stressful. He transferred his business to his two eldest sons, Max and Willie, who had already partly taken over the management of the printing works.

His son, Philip, was summoned from America, so that all his children were with him when he died, peacefully, at his home, Upton Knoll, on the 5th of May, 1902.

John and Elizabeth Bellows,
with their daughter Lucy

EPILOGUE

AFTER JOHN DIED, the family moved from Upton Knoll to Tuffley Lawn, a smaller house near the centre of Gloucester. Quite soon after this, his widow, Elizabeth undertook the editing of his letters, which she did with considerable skill, adding a memoir. The book was published by Kegan Paul, Ternch, Trübner & Co. in 1904 and was twice reprinted. Elizabeth's main interests were her family and her garden, but for many years she served on the Gloucester Board of Guardians and several other committees where her wise counsel was valued. She was cared for by her family, most especially by Hannah and Kitty. In her late eighties, she suffered heart failure and gradually declined in health. She was 91 when she died.

In the four months preceding her death, Elizabeth was looked after by her eldest daughter, Marian, and her husband, Will Waterhouse Gibbins, at their newly-built house, Modewyke, in nearby Brockworth. She and Will lived an uneventful and comfortable life until Will died and Marian moved back into Gloucester where she had maintained links with the printing business and had done useful proof-reading for the Dictionary revisions.

Max, who had married Rose Fox before his father's death, was now managing the printing works with his brother Willie, and he also found time, and had the expertise, to compile the first Bellows German pocket dictionary which was published by Longmans, Green, London in 1916. After the 1914/18 War he worked with War Victims Relief in Germany, helping to set up Quaker projects in various places. His son, Karl, born in 1911, qualified as a surveyor and, after the stationer's shop in the Works was closed, used this knowledge to establish the Map Shop in 1969 in the Commercial Road. He made a late and happy marriage to Margaret Connor, whose cousin now (1993) runs the shop, "Bellows and

Bown", in the same premises. Karl was a member of the John Bellows Board for several years.

Following Max's death in 1932 (the same year as his Mother's) the printing business became Willie's sole responsibility. His love of France and his knowledge of the French language enabled him to make several revisions to the now well-known French/English dictionary. During the first World War, he worked for the Ministry of Propaganda and this brought him friendship with a number of writers, with one of whom, Edmund Gosse, he often holidayed in France. In his fifties, he took up mountaineering. On one occasion, he and his guide climbed the face of the Matterhorn by a new and untried route, and on another he was buried by an avalanche and was saved only by his rescuers finding the handle of his ice-axe sticking above the snow. He remained single, living at Tuffley Lawn until he married Grace Smith when he was 65. For 12 years he was an Alderman of the City of Gloucester.

When Willie died in 1942, his younger brother Jack (John Earnshaw Bellows) took control of John Bellows Ltd. He modernised the business to some extent, as he had had early experience of printing methods, and he became the local President of the British Federation of Master Printers. He also produced the final revised edition of the pocket dictionary in 1951. He had married Olive Hoare, a gifted water-colourist, in 1918, whom he met when he and his sister Hannah had been responsible, with others, for arranging the further education of many young Serbians who were being housed in Cambridge colleges from 1916-1918.

Hannah had graduated with first-class honours at Westfield College. She had studied Russian and History and taught the latter in several schools including The Mount Quaker girls school in York. During the first World War she worked with the Friends War Victims Relief in the Soissons area and in the Vasges. Once she and two of her colleagues were arrested as spies and spent some uncomfortable hours under guard until the French soldiers realised that their prisoners were allies! Later, she transferred to the Serbian Relief Fund, in the Mediterranean area, caring for Serbian refugees and this led to her work in Cambridge. She travelled widely and had a particularly happy holiday in Yugo-Slavia where she was welcomed and given splendid hospitality in Belgrade by the Serbian boys she had known during the War.

Hannah and Kitty lived together surprisingly happily considering the difference in their temperaments. They were both warm and generous and each had her own brand of humour. Hannah became a J.P. and had an interesting public life, whereas Kitty was content with her local friends and with her garden. Just before the first World War, Kitty had lived for two years with May Hughes (the daughter of Thomas Hughes who wrote *Tom Brown's Schooldays*) at the Dewdrop Inn in Whitechapel: this was, literally, a 'drop-in' Centre for local inhabitants.

Kitty wrote several short pieces about her childhood, amongst which was the following, "When we lived at Upton Knoll, one winter my brothers made a long sledge. There were two short seats in front and two taller ones at the back: on each side was a long iron bar resting in a socket, with a hook at the end for guidance and brakes. One time when the half-mile hill outside was frozen and we were travelling down it at a great pace, there was a shout from behind – "DUCK" – and we swept under a horse with a baker's cart attached to it. It was drawn across the side of the road for a rest." This may well have been master-minded by Philip, who later fulfilled his early taste for adventure.

Little is known about this likeable character, or of his life in the United States, other than that he was often on the move. He returned to England to introduce his wife, Edith, to the family, and he came once again later on his own. There was a slight aura of mystery surrounding his name and vague rumours of a roving life; some of the family regarded him as an engaging 'black sheep'.

Lucy was only a year younger than Kitty and these two enjoyed a very close companionship from their childhood onwards. After going to the Gloucester Art School for a year, Lucy then went to Studley Horticultural College: painting in watercolours and gardening were among her abiding interests. She married Henry Cadbury in 1912 and, of course, her life changed considerably. He was the Managing Director of *The Daily News* for some 25 years, and, after his retirement from the paper, he and Lucy became Wardens of Woodbrooke, the Quaker College in Birmingham. He continued to be involved in the newspaper world throughout his life, and he also maintained his youthful enthusiastic interest in agriculture and the countryside. They had five children: their eldest daughter, Betty Hambly, was on the Board of John Bellows Ltd. for several years, and Martin Cadbury, their youngest son, worked at the Eastgate firm to gain experience before setting up his own printing business in Cheltenham.

Dorothy, the youngest in the family, qualified as a doctor during the first World War. After her marriage to Robert Gere, she lived at Mayford in Surrey but travelled regularly to Hackney to run her Mother and Baby Clinic. She, too, was a J.P. locally in Woking. When Jack died in 1955, she courageously, with little knowledge of business, took over the management of John Bellows, Printers, until 1967, when Mr. P. J. Kerr took over the Chairmanship.

Dorothy died in 1972, by which time the directors of John Bellows Ltd. had sold their printing trade to Norman Bros. with an agreement to employ many of the firm's employees. The plant, type, etc., which had not been bought by Norman's was auctioned. The Bellows firm continued trading for a few years until all arrangements with Norman's were completed when, in 1971, the firm went into voluntary liquidation. Later, the valuable site of the Eastgate works was sold and developed.

The publishers of the dictionaries, Longmans, Green, disposed of their diminishing stock (in need of revision), and the Ordnance Survey agency was passed to the Map Shop. Some of Gloucester's older citizens may still remember John Bellows Ltd. which had survived for over a hundred years.

John Bellows: Gloucester Archaeologist

by Malcolm J. Watkins, Archaeology Director, City of
Gloucester Museum

IT IS PROBABLY FAIR to describe John Bellows as the father of
Gloucester Archaeology. Admittedly, Samuel Lysons can claim to
have been the grandfather, but it was Bellows who in modern times
first identified the city wall as a Roman structure, and who began
the serious study of the archaeological heritage of the city, although
in many ways his feet were firmly planted in the dilettante anti-
quarianism of previous generations.

In 1872 he started work on new premises for his steam press on
land between Dog Lane and King Street. This was immediately
north of Eastgate Street, and in line with a section of ancient city
wall to the south of the same cardinal street. Despite the pessimism
of his friend William Lucy (who might claim the title father of
Gloucester geology), he dug down on the site of his new works to
try to establish the presence of the city wall. To his joy he found
the wall as he had hoped, standing for some ten feet (3 metres)
above the water table, and continuing below.

It would be unwise to suggest that Bellows was the first to apply
the principle of stratigraphy to archaeology. It is, on the other hand,
true to say that he was (albeit perhaps less than confidently) apply-
ing the principle before the term 'stratigraphy' was actually first
printed in 1882. This was long before Pitt-Rivers published his
account of work in Cranborne Chase, which is generally accepted
as the earliest published archaeological work to use stratigraphic

techniques effectively. It is not clear from his own accounts whether Bellows recognised different layers in the ground through which he dug, but he correctly deduced that the presence of pottery no later than Roman indicated a Roman date for the city wall.

In this excavation Bellows also demonstrated something which today we still have to demonstrate far too often. Lucy had told him that he was unlikely to find the wall, since it had not been revealed by the foundations of a (now long gone and forgotten) chapel nearby. Whatever may have been the truth on the chapel site, the archaeology remained intact and substantial on the Eastgate House site. In Gloucester at least absence of archaeology does not mean no archaeology.

Some of my earliest, and most treasured, archaeological memories are of the stretch of wall which Bellows uncovered. In a characteristically considerate gesture he kept the wall accessible and visible, albeit in a narrow basement corridor under his printworks. As a young lad, at school in the nearby Rich's I would frequently go in through the little side door from King Street and the staff would give me access to that corridor. I have no idea what they made of it at the time, a pre-teenage boy who seemed to be fascinated by those dank and dark remains, but I am still unable to enter a damp and musty basement or cellar without immediately being transported back to that (at least for me) magical place. It is a sad commentary on our time that today the chamber which succeeded that tunnel is closed and likely to remain so.

In 1873, writing to Professor Max Müller at Oxford, Bellows commented 'Our city is rich in Roman remains, but no systematic account of them is kept'. I like to think that this is one area where things have improved. We, through Gloucester Archaeology, seek to record not only the Roman remains, but also the evidence for other periods in our city's rich heritage. I also like to think that Bellows would be pleased that some, if not all, of the items which he recorded more than a century ago can still be recognised in our public museum collection. I well remember how, at the centenary in 1976 of the Bristol and Gloucestershire Archaeological Society, we were able to show in one case the pottery from Bellows' East Gate investigations alongside the illustrations from the article he wrote for the first transactions. The way in which they were drawn

114

(not by Bellows) and the choice of items for drawing may seem inappropriate to us today, but the fact remains that they are identifiable, which is what archaeological recording must have as one of its underpinning values.

Of course, I would be wrong to view Bellows as infallible; he was the first to admit, and graciously too, that he could make errors. His letter to Müller in February 1877 concerning his lack of access to a copy of Suetonius demonstrates the point. It is, however, more what he omits to say and record than what he does which causes us the greatest problems. I have always been fascinated by the Roman 'soap' which had been found on the East Gate site, but sadly, apart from the mention of it in his letter of 31st March 1873 (again to Müller) no record of it or any analysis has survived to us. By the same token there are many finds from the excavations which are only ascribed to the site, rather than to any particular context. In some instances the context would have helped us in more accurate identification.

One particular find demonstrates this sin of omission more pointedly than any other. In May 1880 Bellows bought from two workmen the unique group of remains found during roadstone quarrying on the Birdlip escarpment. These items, today known as the Birdlip Grave Group, represent a truly amazing assemblage of wealth to be buried with a dead Iron Age princess. She lay, surrounded by her prized possessions, and flanked by two companions, in a stone lined grave. The most striking of the objects is the Birdlip mirror, one of the best survivors of a small number of bronze mirrors with chased and engraved decoration on the rear faces. None of the finds is perfect, but all are remarkably well-preserved. It is possible to argue that the damage was ancient and deliberate, designed to kill ritually the artifacts which were going with the princess into the afterlife. Other items from the grave included: an elaborate silver gilt brooch (the type specimen for a particular group); a little bronze handle modelled on a bull; a massive amber, shale and pyrophillite necklace; and two fine beaten and spun bronze bowls.

One of these bowls had been inverted over the face of the princess, a practice occasionally found in Celtic burials, but both appear to have been functional originally, for the keen eye can make out in

115

the interior the characteristic marks made by a blade cutting something into them. One of the bowls was so fine as to have been pierced by the chuck of the lathe on which it had been spun, but the other shows a distinct punched hole.

The skeletons seem to have been lost – Bellows makes little record of them in his own accounts, but many years after the event a skull, said to be that of the central figure, was discovered in the possessions of a Cheltenham doctor, and returned to reside with the rest of the group.

It is not clear from Bellows' accounts whether the compan-

ions were at head and foot, or side by side with the princess (for such status must be appropriate), nor even which sex they were. It was said at the time that they were male, but it is unwise to assume that such an identification is foolproof. Bellows himself may not have reached the site until a day or two after discovery, so some lack of detail is forgivable: he may have been unable to get answers for himself. Nonetheless, there is no accurate record of the findspot, and consequently it is impossible to pinpoint the location. Such carelessness would today be unforgivable in an archaeologist.

This should not reduce the importance of Bellows' generosity in acquiring the finds and passing them on to the Gloucester City Museum. Several of the items are individually of international importance, and even of international origin. The group as a whole is one of the most important groups of finds from the period immediately prior to the Roman invasion of Britain, and the collection has travelled to Germany and Geneva for exhibitions of Celtic art. The sort of public-spirited local concern which is exhibited by the gift is rarely encountered today for items of such quality; they almost always end up at the

national museums or even on the open market. It is even rarer for a public benefactor to buy an art treasure solely in order to donate it to a public museum.

By modern standards the work done by John Bellows is often infuriatingly vague or uninformative. No sections exist, for example, of the deposits he encountered in his quest for the city wall, although he understood the fundamentals of stratigraphy. In the same way we have an enigmatic reference to a coin of Nero which a carpenter 'picked out of the earth at the end of Mark Street'. By this reference he

117

meant St Mark's Street, but the absence of further details leaves us wondering which end of the street is meant and whether the bank was a last vestige of the defences of the Kingsholm fortress. On the other hand it is probably no more than a field boundary or even the change in ground level between the gravel terrace and the ancient river course.

Bellows was a genuine path-finder. He refused to take for granted the accepted wisdom of his time, but sought to test it; that was how he discovered the Roman wall. Even if today his method seems questionable, his determination is not. But Bellows deserves more recognition that that: he began to break down the barriers between conventional academic thought and popular understanding. His articles speak rather than lecture, and his thoughts lead the reader into interesting little byways; he could, for example, convey a genuine sense of wonder and place over the Neronian coin mentioned above, and the way in which it transported him back to a different era. In these days of a highly developed discipline this sense of wonder is all too often lost to those of us who once enjoyed it, and for whom it was the reason for becoming interested in archaeology.

At its root, however, it is really a reflection of Bellows' interest in people. To him the people of the past could talk to those of the present through the items they had left. In that sense I doubt that Bellows' interest in archaeology is any more than an extension of the rest of his philosophy of life. It is fortunate for Gloucester that he came here rather than somewhere else.

MALCOLM J. WATKINS
January 1993 Archaeology Director
City of Gloucester Museum

The Birdlip grave group, including the Birdlip Mirror, is in the Gloucester Archaeological Museum, as is a small showcase which had belonged to John Bellows, and contains some of his finds. There is, also, a plaque to John Bellows in the City East Gate Viewing Chamber where a section of the Roman Wall can be seen.

A List of John Bellows' Writings

As printed in *John Bellows: Letters and Memoirs*
by Elizabeth Bellows (1904)

Outline Dictionary, for the Use of Missionaries, Explorers and Students of Language. With an introduction by by Professor Max Müller. Title: pp. v-xxxi, and 2-368. Size 6¾ x 4 inches 1867

Ditto ditto. With introductory notes by Professor Summers, on writing Chinese with Roman letters. Title: pp. iii-vi, and 2-368. Size 6¼ x 4 inches 1868

The Bona-fide Pocket Dictionary of the French and English Languages on an entirely new system. Revised and corrected by Auguste Beljame, B.A., Alexandre Beljame, M.A., and John Silbree, M.A. First edition, 6000 copies. References, titles and dedication: pp. i-xvi, and 1-548. Size 41/8 x 25/8 inches 1872

Ditto ditto. Second edition, now in its 80th thousand. Revised by Alexandre Beljame, Docteur-ès-lettres. Proof sheets read by John Sibree, M.A. and Auguste Marrot, B.A. References, title and dedication: pp. i-viii and 1-605: maps. Size 4½ x 2¾ inches 1876

PAMPHLETS, ETC.

Remarks on certain Anonymous Articles designed to render Queen Victoria unpopular 1864

Two Days' Excursion to Llanthony Abbey and the Black Mountains 1868

Ritualism or Quakerism? 1870
Who sent thee to baptize? ... ... ? 1870
The Track of the War around Metz 1871
On the Ancient Wall of Gloucester, and some Roman
    Remains found in proximity to it in 1873. (Proceed-
    ings, Cotteswold Naturalists' Field Club) 1875
Notes on Offa's Dyke: the Black Rock at new Passage:
    Caldicot Castle. (Proceedings C.N.F.C.) 1875
The Roman Wall of Gloucester. (Transactions, Bristol
    and Gloucestershire Archæological Society) 1876
On some Archaeological Remains in Gloucester relating
    to the burning of Bishop Hooper. (Proceedings
    C.N.F.C.) 1878
On some Bronze and other Articles found near
    Birdlip. (Transactions, B.&G.A.S.) ... ... ,,
A Week's Holiday in the Forest of Dean. By Col. Holland
    and John Bellows. This has been frequently re-issued,
    with slight variations form the first edition 1881
Remarks on some Skeletons found at Gloucester in
    1881. (Transactions, B.&G.A.S.) 1882
Chapters of Irish History 1886
Roman Wareham and the Claudian Invasion. (Proceedings,
    Dorset Natural History and Antiquarian Field Club) 1892
William Lucy and his friends of the Cotteswold Club
    five-and-thirty years ago. (Proceedings C.N.F.C.) 1894
On the Past in the Present in Asia. (Proceedings,
    American Antiquarian Society) ... ... ,,
Chisel-drafted Stones at Jerusalem. (Palestine Exploration
    Fund Quarterly Statement, July 1896) 1896
Evolution in the Monastic Orders: Roman Work at
    Chepstow: Roman Remains at Bath. (Proceedings,
    C.N.F.C.) 1898
Survivals of Roman Architecture in Britain. (Proceedings,
    C.N.F.C.) ... ... ,,
The Browns of Bartonbury. (Friends' Quarterly Examiner) 1899
The Forest of Dean. (Proceedings, American Antiquarian
    Society) ... ... ,,
The Romans in Gloucestershire. (Lecture to the Cheltenham
    Natural Science Society) 1900

The Truth about the Transvaal War and the Truth about
  War. (Translations also in French and German) ... 1900
The England of the time of the War of Independence.
  (Proceedings, American Antiquarian Society) ... 1901

ALSO

John Bellows' A Winter Journey to Norway. (John Bellows,
  Gloucester) ... ... Not noted in 1904

BIBLIOGRAPHY

BELLOWS, Elizabeth: *Letters and Memoirs* (Kegan Paul Trench Trübner. 1904)

BELLOWS, Grace: *Life of William Bellows of Gloucester (1873-1942): A Genius for Friendship* (William Sessions Ltd., York. 1982)

BELLOWS, Hannah: *Some Pages of my Life* (John Bellows, Gloucester. 1953)

BELLOWS, John: *Remarks on certain anonymous articles designed to render Queen Victoria unpopular. (1864)*

BELLOWS, John: *A Winter Journey to Norway* (John Bellows, Gloucester. 1867)

BELLOWS, John: *The Track of the War Around Metz* (Trübner & Co.. 1871)

BELLOWS, John and HOLLAND, Col. John: *A Week's Holiday in the Forest of Dean* (John Bellows. 1880)

BELLOWS, John: *The Truth about the Transvaal War & The Truth about War* (John Bellows, Gloucester. 1900)

BELLOWS, John Earnshaw: *John Bellows: Centenary Tribute* (John Bellows, Gloucester. 1931)

BELLOWS, John Earnshaw: *John Bellows and his French Dictionary* (John Bellows, Gloucester. 1948)

BIRKENHEAD, Lord: *500 Best English Letters* (Cassell & Co. London. 1931)

FISHER, H. A. L.: *A History of Europe* (Edward Arnold, London. 1936)

GREENWOOD, John Ormerod: *Quaker Encounters Volume 1. Friends & Relief* (William Sessions Ltd., York. 1975)

HEIGHWAY, Carolyn: *Gloucester, a history and guide* (Alan Sutton. 1985)

HEWISON, Hope Hay: *Hedge of Wild Almonds: South Africa, the Pro-Boers and the Quaker Conscience, 1890-1910* (James Curry Ltd., London. 1989)

NEAVE, Joseph James: *Leaves from the Journal of J. J. Neave* (Headley Bros., London. 1910)

NEWHOUSE, Neville: *A History of the Friends School, Lisburn* (The School Governors. 1974)

SCOTT, Richenda: *Quakers in Russia* (Michael Joseph, London. 1964)

SESSIONS, William K.: *They Chose the Star: Quaker Relief Work in France 1870-1875* (Sessions Book Trust, York. 1991)

The Story of a Pocket Dictionary (from *Printing Times & Lithographers* probably 1877)

Various Letters & Newscuttings from the Bellows Family.

INDEX

ADAMS, James 89-90
Agdam 52*map*, 63, 67
Akara river 52*map*, 65
Albion Cottage 9
Albright, Arthur 29
Allen, Henry *and* family 29
American Antiquarian Society 36-7,
    87, 92
Amesbury (Mass.) 101-2
archaeology 33, 36-7, 42, 87, 88-9,
    92
    Harvard honorary degree 101
    JB's achievements assessed 113-18
    Via Julia 105
Ardouin, Joannin 104
Armenians, Turkish atrocities 89-91
Arnold, Dr Thomas 2
asthma 103

BAILEY, Joshua L. 98
Barclay, Robert, *Apology for the True
    Christian Divinity* 8
Barrett & Sons, printers 6
Bashketchet 52*map*, 68-9
Bassett, John 15
Bazaine, Marshal François 25
Bechuanaland 87-8
Beljame, Professor Alexandre 15
Beljame, Auguste 15
Bellows, Dorothy (daughter of JB)
    44*ill*, 45, 47, 84, 85*ill*, 112
Bellows, [Ebenezer] Forster (brother
    of JB) 2
Bellows, Edith (wife of Philip) 110
Bellows, Elizabeth (*née* Earnshaw;
    wife of JB) 20*ill*, 20-23, 44*ill*,
    85*ill*, 98*ill*, 105*ill*, 108*ill*
    in Bulgaria and Turkey 89-91

    character 106
    and children's games 47-8
    and children's illness 39
    in France and Germany 43-5
    and JB's concern for Stundists 53
    JB's letters published 109
    later career 109
    marriage 20-23
    memoir of JB 93-4, 95, 109
    sailing 84
    in USA 98*ill*, 98-102
Bellows, Hannah (daughter of JB)
    37, 44*ill*, 83*ill*, 85*ill*
    with Doukhabors 82
    later career 109, 110-11
    with Tolstoys 82-3
    at Westfield College 82, 110
Bellows, Hannah (*née* Strickland;
    mother of JB) 1-3
    dies 33
    at Handlow House 21
    illness 21
    with JB in Gloucester 9, 33
Bellows, Dr Henry Whitney
    (American relative of JB) 101
Bellows, John (ancestor of JB) 101
Bellows, John Earnshaw (Jack) (son
    of JB) 43, 44*ill*, 45-7, 70, 84,
    85*ill*
    and 'baker's cart' 45-7
    on JB 106-7
    and JB's letters 106
    later career 110, 112
    at school 91
Bellows, John Thomas (JB) *frontis-
    piece*, 22*ill*, 44*ill*, 55*ill*, 72*ill*,
    85*ill*, 98*ill*, 108*ill*

Bellows' French Dictionary published vii, 14-19, 18-19*ill*
'Bellows Rapid Wages Cylinder' 34-5*ill*, 36
in Bulgaria and Turkey 89-91
character 8, 92, 106-8
  'inconsistencies' 104
childhood 1-2
children 37, 43, 45-50, 51, 106, 111
  born 23, 33, 37, 43, 45
  scarlet fever 39
'errors of judgment' 95-6
Harvard honorary degree 100-101
last illness 102-8
  dies 108
letters 106, 109
  in anthology 50*note*
joins Liberal Unionist Association 42
marriage 20-23, 106
at Metz 23-31, 24*map*, 26*ill*
and neighbours 48-50, 106-7
nervous breakdown 39, 41
loves Norwegian girl 10
in Norway 10-14
occasional publications 36-7
  Home Rule leaflets 42
  religious tracts 36
parents die 33
printing
  apprentice 5-6
  moves to Eastgate House 31, 32*ill*
Quakers
  JB an Elder 89
  JB dissociated from 41, 106
  JB *sits on* Meeting for Sufferings 89
  JB's convincement 8, 104-5, 106
Remarks on Certain Anonymous Articles... 36
and Russian dissidents 53-83
  in Russia 53-70, 71-5, 80
seventieth birthday 97
Track of the War Around Metz published 30-31
Truth about the Transvaal War published 93-6

in USA 98*ill*, 98-102
Week's Holiday in the Forest of Dean, A 37, 92
Winter Journey from Gloucester to Norway, A 10
Bellows, Karl (grandson of JB) 109-10
Bellows, Katharine (Kitty) (daughter of JB) 43, 44*ill*, 84, 85*ill*, 109, 111
Bellows, Lucy (daughter of JB) 43, 44*ill*, 75, 84, 85*ill*, 106, 108*ill*
  later career 111-12
Bellows, Marian (daughter of JB) 33, 44*ill*, 84, 85*ill*, 109
Bellows, Max (son of JB) 31, 43, 44*ill*, 85*ill*, 106
Bellows' German Dictionary 109
  born 23
  death 110
  printing business 108, 109-10
  studies in Leipzig 44
Bellows, Philip (son of JB) 37, 44*ill*, 84, 85*ill*, 108
  lives in USA 97, 98, 102, 106, 111
Bellows, William (Willie) (son of JB) 33, 44*ill*, 85*ill*, 106
  with Doukhabors 79-80
  later career 110
  printing business 108, 109, 110
  with Tolstoys 82-3
Bellows, William Lamb (father of JB) 1-4
  dies 33
  at Handlow House 21
  with JB in Gloucester 9, 33
  opens school at Camborne 4
  teaches at Friends School, Lisburn 2-4
Bevan, Mr (grocer at Liskeard) 1
Bigland, Percy 107
Birdlip, Grave Group 116-17
Birkenhead, 1st Earl of (F.E. Smith), *500 Best English Letters* 50*note*
Blackie, Professor 16
Black Mountains 37
Boer War 93-6

Truth about the Transvaal War published 93-4
Bonet-Maury, Professor 86
Boston (Mass.) 99-100
Bowly, Samuel 9
Bright, John, MP 36, 95-6
Bristol and Gloucester Archaeological Society 36
British Friend (journal) 94*note*
Brockworth, Modewyke 109
Brooks, Edmund Wright 80, 87
Brown, James 61-2
Buchanan (farmer in Manitoba) 82
Bucharest 89
Buckingham, John 36
Bulgaria 89-90

CADBURY, George 78
Cadbury, Henry (husband of Lucy Bellows) 111-12
Cadbury, Martin (son of Lucy Bellows) 112
calculators 34-5*ill*, 36
Camborne 4-6
Campbell, Sir James 92
Canada
  Doukhabors in 78, 79-82, 98
  Hannah Bellows in 82, 83*ill*
capitalism 94-5
Carleton, Colonel 87
Catholicism 41-2
cats 4-5
Chamberlain, Joseph 78, 87-8
children 106, 111
  JB and 37, 43, 45-50, 51
    Freddie Matthews 48-50
    Tolstoys 74-5
China 86
Chinese language, romanization 14
Christian Science 106
Churcham, Handlow House 20-21, 21*ill*, 33
Clitheroe 20, 23
Concord (Mass.) 100
Confucius 104-5
Congrès des Religions à Chicago, Le 86
Connor, Margaret 109
conscientious objection 92, 95
Constantinople (Istanbul) 89, 90-91

Cornish language 14
Cornwall 1*ill*, 1-2, 4-6
  place names 14
  tin mining 60, 87
Cotteswold Naturalists Field Club 36, 37
Cyprus, *and* Doukhabors 78-80
Cyprus Company 78

DAILY Chronicle (newspaper) 77
Daily News (newspaper) 111
Daliar 52*map*, 59, 61
Dean, Forest of 7-8, 37, 92
Devon 84
dictionaries 14
  Cornish 14
  Pocket French vii, 14-17, 18-19*ill*, 45
    Harvard honorary degree 101
    later editions 109, 110
  Pocket German (Max Bellows) 109
  skeleton 14
  romanization of Chinese 14
dog 107
Doukhabors 54, 69, 74, 76-83, 98
Ducie, Lord 106, 107
Dyk 52*map*, 66, 67

EARNSHAW, Elizabeth see Bellows, Elizabeth
Earnshaw, Hugh (brother-in-law of JB) 20
Earnshaw, Mark (father-in-law of JB) 23
Earthorne 2
Edward VII, King, JB visits 97-8
Elementary Education Act, 1870 2
Eliot (Harvard President) 101
Elisabethpol 52*map*, 61, 76
Elkinton, Joseph 80-81, 98
Elkinton, Melinda 98
Elliott, Mary (at Liskeard Meeting) 1
Emerson, Ralph Waldo 43, 92, 100
Evans, William 98
Evelach 52*map*, 63, 67-8

FAST, Herman 55*ill*, 56, 62-3, 67, 71
Forster family (of Bradpole) 2
Forster, William Edward, MP 2
Fox, Rose 109
France
    boursier system 86
    Franco-Prussian War (1870-71) 15, 23-31
    JB holidays in 37-8, 38*ill*, 43-5
Friend (journal) 23
Friends, Religious Society of *see* Quakers

GARDENING 41
Gere, Robert 112
Germany
    book-trade 44-5
    Franco-Prussian War (1870-71) 15, 23-31
    JB holidays in 43-5
    Max Bellows studies in 44
Gerusi 52*map*, 65, 66-7
Gibbins, Will Waterhouse 109
Glen Summit (USA) 99
Gloucester 7-10, 13-23, 30-51, 76-108
    archaeology
        JB's contribution 113-18
        Roman walls 33, 113-15, 117-18
    Art School 111
    Board of Guardians 109
    Commercial Road 9, 109-10
    docks 7, 10
    Eastgate 112
    Friends' Meeting (Greyfriars) 41, 96
        JB an Elder 89
        JB dissociated from 41
    Hoar family 100
    JB employed at 7-9
    JB printing works 9-10
        Eastgate House 31-6, 32*ill*, 84-6
        see also printing
    JB's memorial portrait 107
    Map Shop (Bellows & Bown) 109-10, 112
    match industry 7, 10
    Saint Mary-le-Crypt 95

Tuffley Lawn 109
Via Julia 105
Westgate Street 9-10, 31
Willie Bellows an Alderman 110
Gloucester, Bishop of 36
Gloucester Journal (newspaper) 41, 42, 96
Goodall, Private Joseph 93
Gosse, Edmund 110
Gravelotte (France), battle of 27
Green, James 39
Gregoriowitch (Russian government escort) 63
Grellet de Mabilion, Stephen 2

'H', Captain 13
Hague Peace Conference 91-2, 101
Halifax (Nova Scotia) 79
Hambly, Elizabeth Mary (Betty) 112
Handlow House 20-21, 21*ill*, 33
Harrisons, printers 6
Hartland, Dr Sidney 107
Harvard (Mass.) 104
    JB's honorary degree 100-101
Hilkoff, Prince 68-9, 75, 79
Hoar, Senator George F. 74, 87, 88, 92, 103
    JB visits 99, 100-102
Hoar, John (ancestor of Senator Hoar) 100
Hoar, John (son of Senator Hoar) 100
Hoar, Ruth (wife of Senator George) 99, 101, 103
Hoar, Samuel (nephew of Senator Hoar) 100
Hoare, Olive (wife of Jack Bellows) 110
Hodgkin, Thomas 77
Holland (Netherlands) 91
    Hague Peace Conference 91-2, 101
Holland, Colonel (in Forest of Dean) 37, 92
Holland, William (in Canada) 91, 92, 100
Holmes, Professor Oliver Wendell 17*note*, 51*ill*, 87
    dies 51
    on French dictionary 17

house 99-100
JB writes to
  on breakdown 41
  on children 45-50, 51
  on family reading 43
  on wife in France 44
  in London 45
  on Track of the War... 31
Holmes, Chief Justice Oliver
  Wendell (son of Professor
  above) 88, 99, 102
Home, Bruce 33
Howitt, Armstrong 99-100
Hübner, Dr Emil 42
Hughes, May 111

IRELAND
  Home Rule 41-2
  Lisburn 2-4, 3*ill*

'J', Captain 12
JB *see* Bellows, John Thomas
Jews 94-5
Judd, William 36

KARS 52*map*, 76
Kasbek, Mount 61, 62*ill*
Kedabek 52*map*, 59, 60, 87
Kegan Paul, Tench, Trübner & Co.
  (publishers) 109
Kemp, Caleb 98
Kenworthy, John 76
Kerr, P.J. 112
Khama (Bechuanaland Chief) 87-8
Koura river 52*map*, 64, 68
Kröger, Captain 11-12
Kutais 52*map*, 69

LAKE District 102-3
Lamb, Rev Philip (ancestor of JB) 2
languages 14
  Chinese, romanization 14
  Cornish 14
  French 14-19
  German 109
  linguistic map proposed 42
  Norwegian 10-11
Legge, Professor 86
Leipzig, fair 44-5

Lisburn (N. Ireland), Friends
  School 2-4, 3*ill*
Liskeard 1*ill*, 1-2
London
  Chelsea Embankment 88
  Dewdrop Inn, Whitechapel 111
  JB works in 6
Longmans, Green (publishers) 109
Lord, Arthur 100
Lowell, James Russell 45, 51
Lucien Bonaparte, Prince 16
Lucy, William C. 37
Lydney 88-9

MATTHEWS, Freddie, and family
  48-50
Max Müller, Professor 14-15, 16,
  30, 33
Mennonites 54
Metz (France) 23-31, 24*map*, 26*ill*
  Track of the War... published 30-31
Michell, Francis 44-5
Midland Railway 35*ill*
Miller & Richard, type-casters 16
Milner, Gamaliel 95
mining 60, 87
Molokans 54
Montpesat (France) 37-8, 38*ill*
Morland, Helen 82
Morning Star (newspaper) 36
Moscow, Yasnaya Polyana 72-5,
  73*ill*, 80, 82-3
Müller, Professor *see* Max Müller

NATIONAL Trust 102*note*
nature study 36
Neave, Joseph 53-70, 55*ill*, 71, 79,
  80
Newman, T. 25
Newton, Llewellyn, printer 5-6
Niagara 98-9
Nicholas II, Czar 70, 77, 80-81
  Hague Peace Conference 91
Norman Bros (printers) 112
Norway 10-14, 13*map*
  conscientious objectors 92
Novosti (newspaper) 54
oak trees 92
Oceanic (liner) 102

Ordnance Survey 105, 112
Ovannes (Armenian cook) 90-91

PACIFISM 30-31, 88, 97
  Boer War 94-5
  Doukhabors 76-7
  Stundists 53
patriotism 95
Penington, Isaac 8
Philadelphia 97, 98
philanthropy
  'concerns' 53
  and 'weightier duty' 30
place-names 14, 106
Plymouth (Mass.) 100
Pobedonstov (Russian Church
    Procurator) 54
politics 95
Ponting, Grandfather 48-50
Poti 52*map*, 69
Power, Edward, printer 9, 10
printing 31-6, 32*ill*, 34-5*ill*, 84-6,
    108, 109-10, 112
  Bellows' French Dictionary 15-17,
    18-19*ill*
  French students 86
Prussia *see* Germany
Punch (magazine) 16
puritanism 8, 33, 81-2, 104
Putnam, Elizabeth 88

QUAKERS (Religious Society of
    Friends)
  American 98, 102
  Armenian Relief Fund 89
  and Bechuanaland 87-8
  and Boer War 94-6, 97
  Canada 80
  'concerns' 53
  and Doukhabors 76, 77-81, 98
  and Edward VII's accession 97-8
  JB dissociated from 41, 106
  JB to speak on peace 97
  JB rejoins 89
  JB's children 106
  JB's family connection 2
  JB's religious crisis 8
  JB's religious tracts 36
  Lisburn School 2-4, 3*ill*

Meeting for Sufferings 70
  JB sits on 89
Monthly Meeting 4
Mount School (York) 110
Quaker War Victims' Fund (Fund
    for the Non-Combatant
    Sufferers; Franco-Prussian
    War) 23-30
'Saving Light' 71
Serbian Relief Fund (World War I)
    110-11
star emblem 25
  and Stundists 53-70
United States 78, 80
  and Volga famine 54
War Victims Relief (World War I)
    109, 110
Woodbrooke College 111
Yearly Meeting 53, 91

RAWNSLEY, Canon, *Literary
    Associations in the English Lakes*
    102
reading 6, 8, 43
  Resurrection 81-2
Red Cross, Franco-Prussian War 25
'Redemption Rock' 100
Rhoads, Jonathan 81
Roberts, Private George 93
Roosevelt, Vice-President Theodore
    101
Rowlandson, Mary 100
Rushchuck 89-90
Russia 71-6, 72-3*ill*, 93, 94, 101
  Caucasus 52*map*, 56-70, 62*ill*, 76-
    7, 81, 87
  Doukhabors 54, 60, 69, 74, 76-83
  Mennonites 54
  Molokans 54
  Stundists 53-70, 81
  Volga famine 54

SAINTBRIDGE House 39
St Petersburg 54, 69-70, 72*ill*, 80,
    92, 101
Salisbury, 3rd Marquess of (Prime
    Minister) 42
Schonbeck, Carl (in Sweden) 11
Scotsman (newspaper) 16

Seneca Lake 99
Sessions, Frederick 7-8, 96*ill*, 96
Severn river, railway bridge 39, 40*ill*
Shusha 52*map*, 63-5, 67
Silbree, John 17
Smith, Grace 110
smoking 8
South Africa, Boer War 93-6, 97
Spectator (journal) 16
Strickland, John (grandfather of JB) 2
Studley, Horticultural College 111
Stundists 53-70, 81
Sturge, Wilson 69, 78-9
Summers, Professor 14
Sweden 11, 92

TANGYE family 87
Tartars 60, 61, 63, 67-8
Tchertkoff, Vladimir 76, 77-8, 79, 82, 91
Tiflis 52*map*, 56-9, 62, 68-9, 87
  Doukhabors 76
Times, The (newspaper) 16, 28-9, 76-7
Tolstoy, Count Leo Nikolayevich 56, 69, 71-6, 73*ill*
  and Doukhabors 76-83
  family 71, 73*ill*, 74-5, 80, 81, 82-3
  Resurrection 81-2
  young Bellows visit 82-3
Track of the War Around Metz (JB) 23-31, 24*map*
Trübner and Co., publishers 10, 16, 30
  see also Kegan Paul
Truth about the Transvaal War, The 93-6
Tuffley Lawn 109, 110
Turkey 89, 90-91

Twain, Mark, 'Church of the Gratis Lesson' 17
Two Days' Excursion to Llanthony Abbey and the Black Mountains (JB) 37

UDZHARRI 52*map*, 61-2
United States
  Bellows family connection 101
  Civil War 95-6
  JB *and* Elizabeth in 98*ill*, 98-102
  Philip Bellows lives in 97, 98, 102, 106
  Pilgrim Society 100
  Quakers 98, 102
Upton Knoll 39, 40*ill*, 41, 103-4, 108, 109, 111

VARNA 89, 90
Verigin, Peter 76
Victoria, Queen 36
Virgil 43
Vladikafkas 52*map*, 56

WAGES calculator 34-5*ill*, 36
Wait, stationer and printer 7, 9
Week's Holiday in the Forest of Dean, A (JB *and* Holland) 37, 92
White, Andrew 91-2, 101
Whittier, John Greenleaf 51
  JB at house of 101-2
Whitwell, Thomas 29
Wood, Jessie Ashby 82
Worcester (Mass.) 99

YASNAYA Polyana 72-5, 73*ill*, 80, 82-3

ZABOUCH 52*map*, 65, 67